A CLASS ACT

A CLASS ACT

MUSIC AND LYRICS BY
EDWARD KLEBAN

BOOK BY
LINDA KLINE AND LONNY PRICE

Stage
& Screen

For Ed

The authors wish to thank Marty Bell, Chase Mishkin, Arielle Tepper, Kumiko Yoshi, Robyn Goodman, Lynne Meadow, Barry Grove, Michael Bush, Lee Johnson, Daisy Prince, David Wolf, Grant Sturiale, Eric Stern, Heather Fields, David Bickman, and Steve Cohen. Also, our thanks to Musical Theatre Works and The Manhattan Theatre Club for nurturing *A Class Act*.

INTRODUCTION

It was a long journey from 1993, when I began to catalogue more than a hundred of Edward Kleban's unpublished songs, to the 2001 Broadway production of *A Class Act*, which tells the story of Ed's life, with a score comprised of twenty of the best of these songs.

Who was this songwriter, and why tell his story? Edward Kleban was born in the Bronx in 1939; he wrote the brilliant lyrics for one single Broadway musical, *A Chorus Line*, when he was 36. He won the Tony, the Drama Desk, and the Pulitzer Prize. A dozen years later he died, without ever having another Broadway show.

Was Ed a "one-hit wonder"? Was he spoiled by success? Was he afraid of failure? What kind of person was this guy who wrote "At the Ballet," "Tits and Ass," and "What I Did For Love"? The truth is, Ed even baffled his own friends. In *A Class Act*, Ed's friends gather at his memorial and try to figure him out. Unknown to the friends, the ghost of Ed is present. (Who among us wouldn't love to hear what our friends say at our own memorial?) As the friends look back on his life, Ed gets the chance to help them understand who he really was:

"With all my virtues and my lies

With all the pleasure and the pain around the eyes."

"Self-Portrait," *A Class Act*, Act II, Scene 9

Ed wrote not only the lyrics, but also the beautiful music for "Self-Portrait." He was a gifted composer, and all the music in *A Class Act* as well as the lyrics, are Ed's—with one notable exception. Composer Marvin Hamlisch appears as a character in a scene in which he and Ed struggle to collaborate writing "What I Did for Love" and "At the Ballet" for *A Chorus Line*. The snippets of music in this scene are, of course, Marvin's. *A Chorus Line* director Michael Bennett is another "real" person who appears as a character in *A Class Act*, as is Lehman Engel, who founded and led the BMI Musical Theatre Workshop, where a generation of theater songwriters, including Ed, learned their craft. The friends who tell his story are Ed's fellow students in the BMI Workshop. Are Bobby, Lucy, Charley, Mona, and Felicia real people as well? Well, no. You won't find any of them in the phone book; they don't have social security numbers; they don't pay taxes.

The friends are fictional composites. In "real life" I was a student in Lehman's librettist workshop at BMI. My writing partner, Lonny Price, who is also a director and actor, has worked with innumerable workshop members. Lonny and I invented competitive Charley; sexy, ambitious Mona; loveable, foot-in-his-mouth Bobby, all based on the many aspiring songwriters we've known over the years.

Who is Sophie, Ed's oldest and closest friend, who supports his dreams; who loves him with a full heart; who sets him straight without hurting him? The "real" Ed had several wonderful women in his life, and all their virtues are wrapped up in Sophie. If you don't have a Sophie in your life, you can share ours.

Lonny and I worked on *A Class Act* for six years. At first, we passed drafts of scenes back and forth to each other on floppy disks. The advent of e-mail, a year or so after we began, was a huge help to our collaboration. Most importantly, our fledgling script picked up speed when Lonny became artistic director of Musical Theatre Works, the only developmental theatre in New York devoted exclusively to incubating musicals. We'd have meetings in Lonny's sunny office opposite the Public Theater where *A Chorus Line* began. It felt as if Ed was watching over us, encouraging us to solve seemingly unsolvable problems in the script.

A Class Act was first produced at Manhattan Theatre Club in the fall of 2000. Lonny, who also directed, was "drafted" to play the role of Ed at the last minute. We opened at The Ambassador Theatre on Broadway on Ed's favorite holiday, Valentine's Day, February 14, 2001. The show received five Tony nominations, including Best Musical, Best Book, and Best Score.

Audiences don't say they "enjoyed" *A Class Act*. They don't say they think it's "good." They say, "I love *A Class Act*." A woman came to the box office at The Ambassador and bought tickets when she couldn't get seats to a blockbuster Broadway show. She laughed and cried, and came back seven times. Our first "groupie." We had a number of teenagers who became *Class Act* "groupies." They'd wait for "Sophie" and "Lucy" and "Bobby" outside the stage door night after night. I think that they were "turned on" by the window into a world of songwriting far removed from MTV. Maybe a few of them will be inspired to carry on the tradition of writing for the musical theater.

As I write this, *A Class Act* is in rehearsal for its first post-Broadway production, at Pasadena Playhouse. In July, we will have our first international production, in Tokyo, fittingly, at The Act Theatre. Williamson Music, a division of Rodgers & Hammerstein, is publishing a book of vocal selections. And with this Stage & Screen edition, *A Class Act* is now available in print.

When you read *A Class Act*, you'll have a unique opportunity to look closely at the craft in Ed Kleban's lyrics. As Lucy says when she first hears "Paris Through the Window," "there's not a false rhyme, not a missed stress." Ed's words are as natural as conversation, as heightened as poetry. Few new musicals make it from the page to a commercial production. A handful make it to Broadway. Lonny and I are grateful that *A Class Act* was one of them. It was a story we had to tell. The songs needed to be heard. We had to do what Ed was unable to do in life. We hope we did him proud.

Linda Kline
April 30, 2002

CHARACTERS

Actor 1
ED KLEBAN: An aspiring songwriter. Charming and vulnerable. He wears his phobias and his affections on his sleeve.

Actor 2
SOPHIE: Ed's first love. A doctor. She has great warmth and intelligence. Grounded and wry.

Actor 3
LEHMAN ENGEL: The leader of the BMI Musical Theatre Workshop. Sophisticated, distinguished, and most importantly, a father figure to his students. Southern, Jewish, gay.

Actor 4
BOBBY: A drummer and aspiring songwriter. He may have some rough edges, but he is Ed's loyal and loving friend.

MICHAEL BENNETT: The charismatic choreographer and director. Machiavellian and brilliant.

Actor 5
CHARLEY: An aspiring songwriter. Ivy League, talented, competitive, and somewhat pretentious.

MARVIN HAMLISCH: The composer, at age 29. Talented, energetic. As outgoing as Ed is introverted.

DR. NODINE, a psychiatrist; JEAN-CLAUDE CHEVRAY

Actor 6
LUCY: A singer in Broadway musicals. Later, Ed's girlfriend. Sweet natured; a "giver." Perhaps too nice for the theatre.

TAP DANCE STUDENT; GIRL 1; CHORUS of "A Chorus Line"

Actor 7
FELICIA: An aspiring songwriter. Later, a music industry executive. Glamorous, confident. A powerhouse. Ambitious to be "The First Woman Who…"

GIRL 2; TAP DANCE STUDENT; CHORUS of "A Chorus Line"

Actor 8
MONA: An aspiring songwriter. Seductive and kittenish. She has a small talent, and is attracted to men who can further her career.

CHORUS of "A Chorus Line"

SCENES & MUSICAL NUMBERS

Act I

Scene 1: The Shubert Theatre, 1988
"*Light On My Feet*" .... Ed with Company

Scene 2: Hillside Hospital, 1958
"*Beside the Fountain in Garden of the Hospital*" ..... Company
"*One More Beautiful Song*" .... Ed with Sophie

Scene 3: The Shubert Theatre, 1988

Scene 4: The BMI Musical Theatre Workshop
"*Fridays At Four*" .... Company
"*Bobby's Song*" .... Bobby
"*Charm Song*" .... Lehman
"*Paris Through the Window*" ..... Ed with Bobby and Charley

Scene 5: Ed's Apartment, 1966
"*Mona*" .... Mona
"*Under Separate Cover*" .... Lucy, Sophie, and Ed

Scene 6: Recording Studio/Columbia Records, 1966-1971
"*Don't Do It Again*" .... Felicia with Ed
"*Gauguin's Shoes*" .... Ed and Company
"*Don't Do It Again*" reprise .... Lehman

Scene 7: Columbia Records, 1972

Scene 8: Outside The Royal Alexandra Theatre, Toronto, 1972
"*Light On My Feet*" reprise.................. Ed and Bobby
"*Follow Your Star*" .... Sophie and Ed

Act II

Scene 1: The Shubert Theatre, 1988; Manhattan, 1973
"*Better*" .... Ed, Felicia, and Company

Scene 2: Sophie's Laboratory, 1973
"*Scintillating Sophie*"............................... Ed
"*The Next Best Thing to Love*" .... Sophie
"*Light On My Feet*" reprise .... Ed

Scene 3: Central Park, 1973

Scene 4: Michael Bennett's Studio, 1973
"*Broadway Boogie Woogie*"......................... Lucy

Scene 5: The Public Theater, 1974-75
"*A Chorus Line*" Excerpts...................... Company

Scene 6: Manhattan, 1975-1985
"*Better*" reprise .... Ed and Company
"*I Choose You*"............................. Ed and Lucy
"*The Nightmare*".................................. Ed

Scene 7: Sophie's Laboratory, 1985
"*Say Something Funny*" .... Company

Scene 8: The BMI Musical Theatre Workshop, 1986
"*I Won't Be There*"................................. Ed

Scene 9: St. Vincent's Hospital, 1987
"*Self Portrait*"..................................... Ed

Scene 10: The Shubert Theatre, 1988
"*Self Portrait*" reprise........................ Company

PRODUCTION HISTORY

The Kleban Project, later called *A Class Act,* was developed in workshops at Musical Theatre Works, a not-for-profit theater at which co-author Lonny Price is the artistic director. *A Class Act* had its premiere production at The Manhattan Theatre Club, in the fall of 2000. After a sold-out run, the show moved to The Ambassador Theatre on Broadway on Valentine's Day, 2001. Opening night was March 13, 2001.The producers were Marty Bell, Chase Mishkin, and Arielle Tepper. *A Class Act* received five Tony nominations, including Best Musical, Best Score, and Best Book. The score also received Off-Broadway's Obie Award, and a Drama Desk nomination.

Pasadena Playhouse presented the first regional production in the spring of 2002. The first international production was at The Akasaka Act Theatre in Tokyo, produced by Tokyo Broadcasting System, in July 2002. Several regional productions are scheduled for the 2002-2003 season.

RCA recorded the Manhattan Theatre Club production of *A Class Act,* and vocal selections have been published by Williamson Music, a division of Rodgers and Hammerstein. Stock and amateur rights to productions of *A Class Act* are available through Rodgers and Hammerstein.

The Broadway production of *A Class Act* featured the following cast:

LUCY . . . . Donna Bullock
BOBBY, MICHAEL . . . . . David Hibbard
ED . . . . Lonny Price
FELICIA . . . . Sara Ramirez
LEHMAN . . . . Patrick Quinn
CHARLEY, MARVIN . . . . Jeff Blumenkrantz
MONA . . . . Nancy Kathryn Anderson
SOPHIE . . . . Randy Graff

Director: Lonny Price
Choreography: Marguerite Derricks
Set Design: James Noone
Costume Design: Carrie Robbins
Lighting Design: Kevin Adams
Sound Design: Acme Sound Partners
Orchestrations: Larry Hochman
Music Direction: David Loud
Incidental Music: Todd Ellison
Production Stage Manager: Jeffrey M. Markowitz
Stage Manager: Heather Fields
Associate Director: Stafford Arima

DIRECTOR'S NOTE

In terms of the physical production, I think the piece is served best by a minimum of scenery and props, so that scene changes can happen as quickly as a lighting cue. If projections are available, they seem to be a nifty solution in defining locale. The trickier aspects of the show lie in its multiple realities.

The show takes place at the Shubert Theatre in New York in 1988 at Ed Kleban's memorial. The ghost of Ed, having heard his friends speak about him in a way he believes to be inaccurate, tries to justify his life by conjuring up events from his past to show his friends (and the memorial audience) his life as he saw it. The bulk of the show switches from the memorial to these flashbacks of Ed's life. A third reality involves Sophie, Ed's best friend, who interrupts the ghost's telling of his life to try and keep him on track. The final reality occurs at crucial moments in the show, when the ghost of Ed hears his friend's voices arguing about him, misunderstanding him, which drives Ed crazy.

The truth is, in the playing, all of this makes sense. However, the more the director can clarify these realities, the better. Linda Kline and I have tried to make clear in the stage directions exactly what is going on. We hope we've been successful.

Lonny Price, January 14, 2002

ACT I

SCENE 1

THE STAGE OF THE SHUBERT THEATRE, BROADWAY

FEBRUARY 1988

(House lights down. The stage is in total darkness. We hear:

Music: FANFARE.

LIGHTS click on the empty stage of the Shubert Theatre to reveal
LUCY, *pretty, about 40, onstage alone, in quiet contemplation. She*
wears a winter coat; a canvas L.L. Bean-type bag is at her feet. A
pedestal is placed downstage left.

After a beat, BOBBY *enters, eating a donut. Although also in*
his 40s, he is boyish: not quite a "grown-up.")

BOBBY: Sorry, Lucy, I love hanging out backstage.

LUCY: Yeah, the glamor!

BOBBY: No, the donuts. Did you know that since *A Chorus
          Line* opened here, they've gone thru 6,438 boxes?

LUCY: Well, considering that Ed probably wrote about that
          many drafts for every lyric in the show, it sounds
          pretty fair to me.

BOBBY: Who'd have thought *A Chorus Line* would outlive Ed?

LUCY: Not Ed, I'll tell you that. *(Beat)* It feels weird being
          here without him.

BOBBY: (*Reassuringly*) I know.

LUCY: (*Taking a notepad from her pocket*) Hey, let's check the
            list of speakers. You're gonna tell the baseball story.

BOBBY: Right. Marvin's gonna tell about when he and Ed
            wrote the songs for *A Chorus Line*. And you, Luce?

LUCY: Bobby—I know just what I'm going to say. People
            will be getting to the theater soon. C'mon, give me a
            hand with Ed.

(LUCY *picks up the canvas bag by the handles.*)

BOBBY: You mean he's—

LUCY: (*A yes*) Uh-huh.

(BOBBY *takes a Wedgwood urn from the bag, which is actually
the English Olivier Award Ed won for* A Chorus Line. *He holds it
up carefully.*)

BOBBY: With his claustrophobia, he must be dying in there.

LUCY: Oh, Bobby.

(BOBBY *places the urn on the pedestal.*)

BOBBY: Hey, I'm telling you, this memorial is going to be ter-
            rific. If it wasn't for Ed being dead, he wouldn't have
            missed it.

LUCY: Bobby—

BOBBY: Oh God, what a thought, Ed at his own memorial.
            I'm going backstage to find a place for the coats. I'll
            be right back.

(BOBBY *exits with* LUCY'*s coat.* LUCY *remains onstage, collecting her thoughts. She crosses to the pedestal as the orchestra begins to play softly...a ghostlike tremolo.*

Unseen by LUCY, *the urn begins to glow with light. The music builds, the light grows larger, becoming a spotlight which begins to travel across the stage, finally settling on a seat in the audience where a dapper, bespectacled man is seated, watching the show. The light has materialized the ghost of* ED KLEBAN. ED *turns to the audience member seated next to him, and strikes up a conversation:)*

ED: I THOUGHT I'D DROP BY
TO HEAR THE PEOPLE GUSHING—
'CAUSE AFTER YOU DIE,
THEY ALWAYS GET YOU BLUSHING . . .

*(*ED *gets up from his seat and walks to the stage.)*

SO I'VE MADE A THORNTON WILDER RETURN!
GIVE ME A GOOD, GUSHY GOODBYE—
'CAUSE EVEN INSIDE OF AN URN

(He begins to do a softshoe, unseen by Lucy.)

I STAY LIGHT ON MY FEET
I STAY LIGHT ON MY FEET
AND GIVE 'EM THAT
DAH-DAH-DAH-DAH
DAH-DAH-DAH-DAH
DAH-DAH-DAH-DAH . . .

BOBBY (OS): Lucy, wait'll you see this!!

(A huge poster of ED KLEBAN, *dapper in a suit and tie, standing in front of the* Chorus Line *marquee outside the Shubert Theatre flies in.* ED *admires the picture of himself as* BOBBY *re-enters.)*

ED: I STAY LIGHT ON MY FEET
           I STAY LIGHT ON MY FEET
           AND HIT 'EM WITH
           SHU-DAH-BU-DWAH
           SHU-DAH-BU-DWAH
           SHU-DAH-BU-DWAH . . .

LUCY: *(pointing to the picture)* Oh my God! I gave him that tie!

ED: WHEN DAME FORTUNE TOSSES ME A CURVE
           I NEVER GIVE AWAY TO DESPAIR
           I HANG ON WITH EV'RY LITTLE NERVE
           TRYIN' TO KEEP MY BALANCE AS I DANGLE IN
           AIR . . .

(FELICIA, *a glamorous music executive, enters grandly, in Armani and a fur cape. The ghost of* ED, *"invisible," enjoys watching his friends arrive.*)

LUCY: Felicia!

FELICIA: *(She sees the poster)* Oh, that's just too tragic!

LUCY: So young . . .

FELICIA: Oh, well, yes, but I was talking about the tie.

ED: I LAND RIGHT ON MY FEET
           I LAND RIGHT ON MY FEET
           AND GO WITH THAT
           DAH-DAH-DAH-DAH
           DAH-DAH-DAH-DAH
           DAH-DAH-DAH . . .

LUCY: Felicia—you and Ed had so much history. I hope we can be friends.

FELICIA: Don't you have your own friends?

(FELICIA *turns from* LUCY *and approaches the urn.*)

ED: FLAT-FOOT FLOOGIES FINISH UP LAST
MOST OF THEM ARE LIVING ON SPAM

FELICIA: . . . to think in this blizzard I had to take the subway!
"What I Did for Love."

ED: THAT'S WHY LIGHT ON MY FEET
IS WHAT I AM!

(CHARLEY *enters, wearing an Ivy League tweed jacket. A song-writer, 40s, a Yale man, a bit of a snob. He is followed by* LEHMAN ENGEL, *60s, distinguished, a Broadway conductor and teacher of songwriting in the BMI Musical Theatre Workshop.*)

CHARLEY: Lehman!

LEHMAN: Charley! *(Looking at urn)* He was my best student.

CHARLEY: I thought I was your best student.

ED: AND GIVE 'EM THAT
DAH-DAH-DAH-DAH
DAH-DAH-DAH-DAH
DAH-DAH-DAH-DAH . . .

(MONA *enters. She is sexy in a kittenish way.*)

MONA: Felicia!

FELICIA: Mona!

(MONA *and* FELICIA *"air kiss" as* LUCY *observes.*)

MONA: Hey, come to the reading of my new show!

FELICIA: You've been writing that show for twenty years.

MONA: Ed said I was talented.

FELICIA: At what?

ED: AND HIT 'EM WITH
            SHU-DAH-BU-DWAH
            SHU-DAH-BU-DWAH
            SHU-DAH-BU-DWAH . . .

MONA: I'm gonna miss him playing his songs.

LEHMAN: The tenth draft . . .

MONA: The twentieth draft . . .

LEHMAN: He was a perfectionist.

BOBBY: Hey! Me, too! It's what's been holding me back for years!

CHARLEY: Hey, Mona, did Ed ever tell you what he thought of me?

MONA: Oh, really, Charley! I don't think Ed ever thought of you.

BOBBY: My best friend. Played drums on his demo tapes—I've always spent too much time helping friends. It's what's been holding me back for years!

ED: DAH-DAH-DAH-DAH
            DAH-DAH-DAH-DAH
            DAH-DAH-DAH—

CHARLEY: People say AIDS.

LUCY: Never!

MONA: He was straight. I know.

ED: FLAT-FOOT FLOOGIES FINISH UP LAST
            MOST OF THEM ARE LIVING ON SPAM

CHARLEY: No one who writes a hit musical is straight.

BOBBY: It's what's been holding me back—

ALL (EXCEPT ED):
            (affectionately)—for years!

ED: THAT'S WHY LIGHT ON
            MY FEET IS WHAT I AM!
            TIME NOW FOR SINGIN' MY PRAISES—
            I'M HERE TO DRINK IT IN.
            HIT ME WITH FLATTERING PHRASES—
            IT'S GONNA BE SWEET,
            GONNA BE SWEET,
            LET IT BEGIN!

(THE COMPANY *talk about* ED *to each other. The ghost of* ED, *unseen, listens for their loving compliments.*)

CHARLEY: Where's Sophie?

BOBBY: Ed forbid her to come.

LEHMAN: There was that thing between them.

MONA: He cut Sophie out.

FELICIA: C'mon guys, the minute we met Ed in class, we knew
            HE . . . HE WAS CRAZY . . .

LEHMAN: HE WAS MAD'NING,

FELICIA: SHORT AND BALD.

MONA: But kinda sexy.

ED: Thank you.

COMPANY: HE—HE BURNED WITH AMBITION,
BUT AFTER HE MADE IT,
HE GOT STALLED.

ED: Hey guys, this is my memorial!

GROUP 1:   HAD A LIST OF PHOBIAS
THAT ANYONE WITH PHOBIAS
WOULD ENVY—

GROUP 2:   EVERYTHING WITH EDDIE WOULD BE ON
AND OFF
AND ON AND
OFF AGAIN . . .

COMPANY: HE—

LEHMAN: He wasted his potential.

GROUP 2:   HE WAS DRIVEN.

GROUP 1:   —HE COULD CHARM YOU,

COMPANY: HE COULD SCALD.

LUCY: YOU COULD SAY YOU KNEW HIM IF YOU
KNEW HIM
(BUT YOU KNEW THAT YOU WERE GUESSING)

LEHMAN: SOMEONE WHO WAS TERRIFIED OF FAILURE
AND SUSPICIOUS OF SUCCESS—

ED: Oh, I get it—
           THEY'RE JUST STRICKEN WITH GRIEF—
           THEY'RE JUST STRICKEN WITH GRIEF—

MONA: HE'D BE SUCH A PUSSYCAT,

BOBBY: AND THEN HE'D SNAP
           LEAVE YA HANGIN'

COMPANY: FOR HIS GODDAMN NAP!

ED: THIS IS BEYOND BELIEF
           THIS IS BEYOND BELIEF!

CHARLEY: HE WAS UNFULFILLED,

WOMEN: HE WAS FILLED WITH DOUBT—

COMPANY: HE WAS MORE THAN ED COULD EVER
           FIGURE OUT.
           AND HE DROVE US CRAZY—
           HE ENRAGED AND HE ENTHRALLED!
           SCARED OF EV'RYTHING—
           SO NEUROTIC
           AND TEMPERAMENTAL—
           A HYPOCHONDRIAC!
           AFTER *CHORUS LINE*
           SOMETHING HAPPENED,
           'CAUSE AFTER *CHORUS LINE*
           NOTHING HAPPENED!

   (The music builds manically)

           AFTER *CHORUS LINE*
           AFTER *CHORUS LINE*
           AFTER *CHORUS LINE*
           AFTER *CHORUS LINE*
           AFTER *CHORUS LINE*
           AFTER *CHORUS LINE*

ED: STOP!

(The COMPANY *freezes, scattered about the stage with* ED *in the center. Each is in a separate* LIMBO.*)*

I can't believe this! I know you can't hear me, but come on, I'm dead! You're my friends—isn't anybody gonna say something nice about me? You know, like how adorable and funny I was . . . ? At times . . . ? Sometimes . . . ?

(As before, they do not hear the ghost of ED, *but unfreeze for each of their lines, responding as though they were in a conversation with each other about him.)*

ED: Bobby?

BOBBY: The money ruined him!

ED: It was never about money! It was the work!

MONA: Too selfish to have kids!

ED: How'd you like me for a father?

FELICIA: Didn't get what he wanted.

ED: Who says?

LEHMAN: Wasted his potential—

ED: I wrote hundreds of songs.

CHARLEY: He was blocked.

ED: I wrote hundreds of songs! I can't believe this. You didn't get it! You didn't get me! For God's sake, it's all in the songs! Just listen to my songs!

(LUCY *begins to address the memorial audience. A "speaker's podium" is established by a golden rectangle of light—there is no actual piece of furniture.*)

LUCY: Good afternoon everyone, I'm Lucy Chaplin . . .

ED: Thank God, Lucy—set it straight.

LUCY: *(Continuing, without hearing the ghost of Ed)* . . . Welcome to the Shubert Theatre, where tonight Ed's musical, *A Chorus Line*, will play its five thousand, two hundred and thirteenth performance.

ED·   Now, that's true.

LUCY: I know Ed would be so pleased to see all of you here today.

ED: Well, most of you. Get the hair out of your eyes, Luce.

LUCY: *(Not hearing Ed, she doesn't adjust her hair)* We all have Ed stories.

ED: Yes. Good ones.

LUCY: Okay, so here goes. Ed grew up in the Bronx, in the forties. Yankee Stadium was nearby, and Eddie used to leave the window open, just in case a fly ball flew in.

ED: Embarrassing, but true.

LUCY: That never happened, but he did end up with three parakeets, a canary, and a Java temple bird.

ED: Right. Hair, Luce.

(*She "hears"* ED *subliminally, and adjusts her hair.* ED *beams.*)

LUCY: Eddie was ten when his parents dragged him to his
            first Broadway musical, *South Pacific.*

ED: In my itchiest pants.

LUCY: He was so crazy about it, the next day, he taught the
            Java temple bird to sing the entire score.

ED: And she was the best damn Bloody Mary I ever saw.

(MUSICAL STING)

*(LUCY continues in mime. The MEMORIAL LIGHT dims to half,
as SOPHIE enters in LIMBO, seen only by ED. She is ED's friend
from childhood: smart, warm, wry.)*

LIMBO

SOPHIE: Hi, Eddie.

ED: Sophie, go away. I'm not talking to you.

SOPHIE: Since I'm here, I must be on your mind.

ED: Traitor! Benedict Arnold! Tokyo Rose!

SOPHIE: We've been friends since third grade. I'm part of the
            story.

ED: Yeah and with friends like you ...

SOPHIE: You want them to get you? You gotta tell the truth—
            all of it. From the start.

ED: Okay, fine. I'll start with the opening night of *A
            Chorus Line.*

SOPHIE: Hillside Hospital.

(*MUSIC:* "Fountain in the Garden" *figure*)

ED: The looney bin? Are you nuts? Why do they have to see that? I was 18. Ancient history. The Peloponnesian Wars.

SOPHIE: Your war, Eddie—

ED: No, I can't do this.

SOPHIE: What about the truth?

ED: I'm trusting you here.

SCENE 2

HILLSIDE HOSPITAL, 1958

(The garden of a mental hospital. There is a bench downstage.

Five PATIENTS *(*COMPANY*) enter and sing as a Greek chorus.* DR. NODINE *enters and crosses to* ED *with a paper for him to sign.)*

PATIENTS: BESIDE THE FOUNTAIN IN THE GARDEN OF
    THE HOSPITAL
WE USED TO SIT
WE USED TO TALK

BESIDE THE FOUNTAIN IN THE GARDEN OF
    THE HOSPITAL
WE'D TRY TO CRAWL
SO WE COULD WALK
WE USED TO WONDER WHETHER JEFF

WOULD JUMP THE FENCE
AND BELT A FEW
OR IF JEANETTE WAS BACK ON THORAZINE,
OR ONLY FEELIN' BLUE
BESIDE THE FOUNTAIN IN THE GARDEN OF
    THE HOSPITAL
WE THOUGHT WE KNEW . . .

(DR. NODINE *exits, followed by four of the* PATIENTS. *The* FIFTH PATIENT *sits on a bench.* SOPHIE, *now 18 and a college coed, enters.*)

SOPHIE: Hi, Eddie.

ED: Ah, Sophie—the debutante from Bryn Mawr!

SOPHIE: *(Mispronouncing it mockingly, so it rhymes with "plant")* "Debutante."

ED: I'll bet Katharine Hepburn didn't make Dean's List at Bryn Mawr.

SOPHIE: Matter of fact, I think she did.

ED: She's in good company. My first day with visiting privileges. I'm glad you came.

SOPHIE: Are you kidding? Who else would ask me on a date to a mental hospital?

ED: You're a lucky girl.

(ED *and* SOPHIE *approach the bench where* THE FIFTH PATIENT *is seated. The* PATIENT *exits. There's a beat.*)

ED: You weren't scared coming in here?

SOPHIE: I wasn't?

ED: *(Confidentially—a secret)* Yeah, well, everyone here is a little touched.

SOPHIE: *(Pause)* We don't have to talk about it.

ED: You mean you're willing to pass up the opportunity to hear what it was like when the first boy you made out with flipped his kugel and jumped into the looney bin?

SOPHIE: You're right. Tell me everything. Was it . . . ?

ED: Extremely. At first, they thought I might be catatonic. They gave me shock treatment.

SOPHIE: Oh, God.

ED: It has its upside. Now if I put my finger on the TV antenna, I get much better reception on Channel 11.

SOPHIE: Why didn't you tell me?

ED: I guess I was—I just couldn't.

SOPHIE: So what happened?

ED: Last semester, I started having these—thoughts. Scary thoughts. Nuclear bomb attacks. Certain dark cloud formations. One day I woke up in my dorm, and thought, what if I started screaming in class and couldn't stop.

SOPHIE: So—

ED: So I stopped going to classes. In the end, it got so bad, I was afraid to talk. And one day, I couldn't. And— *(He stops)*

SOPHIE: And—

ED: And, that's when my parents brought me—*(Just reliving it, he can't talk)*

SOPHIE: Here.

ED: *(Recovering—pulling himself back into the present)* Yeah. It's not so bad really. We play a lot of Crazy Eights—

SOPHIE: Eddie!

ED: And I have this great doctor. Dr. Nodine. But even on the couch with Dr. Nodine, I couldn't talk. I'd think my mother would kill me if I was on the couch with my shoes on, but I couldn't even get the words out to say that.

SOPHIE: God, Eddie.

ED: Two weeks of him looking at me, me looking at him, him looking at me. Finally, he snapped.

SOPHIE: So what happened?

(ED runs to the piano and moves it into the playing area with SOPHIE. The piano will remain on stage throughout the play: it is Ed's lifeline to sanity.)

ED: He brought me to the dining room, and showed me this old piano pushed up against the wall with one of those brown cover things on it. And every morning, after breakfast, when they're clearing the tables, I come here and I start to play.

(He begins to play "One More Beautiful Song," first with one finger, then more, until he plays with both hands.)

At first, I played everything I ever knew ... over and over—all the pieces I'd ever practiced ... and before I knew it, my fingers began taking on a mind of their own ... and I realized that what I was playing was actually mine. And more than that, I wasn't scared anymore ... Voices in my head started to fit words to the music.

SOPHIE: Are you telling me this music is ... ?

ED: Yes, Sophie! Mine! I needed you to be the first person to hear it. Oh, Soph, all I want is ...

LET THERE BE ONE MORE BEAUTIFUL SONG
IN THE COSMOS
LET THERE BE ONE MORE PERFECTLY
RAVISHING TUNE
LET THERE BE WORDS THAT SIMPLY SAY
THE WAY I FEEL TODAY
THREE QUARTERS CHURCH ... ONE QUARTER
... A SALOON
LET THERE BE ONE HUGE LAUGH BEFORE IT'S
OVER
AND MAYBE ONE HIGH NOTE TO CRACK THE
DOME
LET THERE BE ONE MORE BEAUTIFUL SONG
THIS LOVELY
EV'NING
(ED *improvises*)—AND—DAH, DAH, DAH, DAH ...
I haven't finished the ending. What do you think?

SOPHIE: I love it.

ED: You do?

SOPHIE: I do!

ED: Oh, Soph, that's so ... Soph, I love writing songs. I love hearing them when they're finished. I love that once I get them right, I can go back the next day, and they're still there … Writing music, Sophie, writing music makes me sane… and every day, I can't wait to get to the piano to write more…

SOPHIE: *(Genuinely thrilled for him)* God, Eddie!

ED: Dr. Nodine thinks I'm ready to leave. But I can't go back to Columbia and become a lawyer who only plays piano at parties. My head's throbbing—I'm gonna have a stroke.

SOPHIE: It's just a headache. Get an aspirin.

(ED *reaches into his pocket and gets a cigarette.* SOPHIE *pulls the cigarette out of his mouth.*)

SOPHIE: That's a cigarette!

ED: I want to be a songwriter. I want to write songs that tell stories—like in *South Pacific.*

SOPHIE: *West Side Story!*

ED: Yeah, you think I'm nuts? Truth.

SOPHIE: Truth? Well, sure—But that matters for a lawyer—not for a songwriter—

ED: You think?

SOPHIE: Do it.

ED: How'll I make a living?

SOPHIE: Do it, Eddie.

ED: What if it turns out I'm not as good as I think I might be?

SOPHIE: Do it, Eddie. You at Columbia becoming a Broadway
           songwriter; me at Bryn Mawr becoming Madame
           Curie!

ED: Bryn Mawr! Oh God, the spelling of that school
           alone thrills me!

           I THINK I'LL PUT MY TONY IN THE FOYER
           NO, THAT IS MUCH TOO PUSHY . . .

SOPHIE: WE'LL HAVE A DEN!

ED: AND THANK YOU MR. GLICKENHOUSE FOR
           THE HELP WITH ADVERBS . . .

ED & SOPHIE:
           AND HERE WE GO AGAIN . . .
           LET THERE BE ONE HUGE LAUGH BEFORE IT'S
               OVER
           AND MAY THE LONG HIGH NOTE BE HEARD IN
               ROME
           LET THERE BE ONE MORE BEAUTIFUL SONG
           THIS LOVELY EV'NING

ED: AND THEN . . .

(Trying to finish writing the lyric as he sings)

           WE'LL ALL . . .

SOPHIE: GO HOME?

ED: Perfect! Sophie, when I'm rich and famous and a lit-
           tle less crazy will you marry me?

SOPHIE: Oh, Eddie.

TOGETHER: AND THEN WE'LL ALL GO HOME.

(They kiss as the LIGHTS black out. SOPHIE *exits slowly, as* ED *watches, as if in a dream.)*

SCENE 3

THE MEMORIAL, 1988

(LIGHTS pop on revealing LEHMAN *speaking at the memorial.* ED *listens.)*

LEHMAN: As many of you know, my name is Lehman Engel. And Ed was like a son to me.

ED: Aw, Lehman.

LEHMAN: Back in the sixties, I planned to give a six-month course in writing musicals, but it's been over twenty years—and the students in the BMI Musical Theatre Workshop refuse to leave.

(Addressing MONA *and* CHARLEY *in the audience at the memorial)*

ED: Right, Mona? Charley? The class has become a family. I know I could always count on you to be accurate.

LEHMAN: No one in the workshop wanted to write musicals more than Ed. But at twenty-four, he needed to make a living—and his talent helped him land a plum job as a producer at Columbia Records.

ED: Truth is: nepotism. Cousin Norman ran the Columbia Record Club.

LEHMAN: His boss was my good friend Goddard Lieberson, a brilliant record executive. And he started Ed off producing these choice dance records.

ED: Not my choice...

(LIGHTS go to half on LEHMAN *as an intercom buzzer buzzes.)*

GODDARD (OS):
Kleban!

ED: Yes, Mr. Lieberson?

GODDARD (OS):
Good work on the "Polkas for Lovers" record.

ED: Thanks, Mr. Lieberson. Next, I'd really like to try something different.

GODDARD (OS):
Different? You got it! How about "Cha Cha for Lovers"?

(LIGHTS back up on LEHMAN*)*

LEHMAN: Ed and Goddard worked very closely together—
(LEHMAN *continues in mime, under)*

ED: Closely, Lehman? I never saw him! My office was on the fourth floor—his was on the twenty-fourth and, I'm not saying elevators are unsafe, but why do those little red buttons say "in case of emergency...?"

LEHMAN: One thing for sure, Ed loved that job.

(ED groans eloquently. LIGHTS out on LEHMAN.*)*

SCENE 4

NYC LIMBO/BMI WORKSHOP, 1966

ED: MONDAY AT NINE ...
           OFF TO THE OFFICE
           MONDAY AT SIX ...
           BACK FROM THE OFFICE
           TUESDAY AT NINE, MORE OF THE SAME, ALAS!
           BUT—
           FRIDAY AT FOUR
           FRIDAY AT FOUR
           LEHMAN'S DIVINE MUSICAL COMEDY CLASS ...

(MONA enters as she was in 1966, in her 20s. She wears a mini dress and go-go boots.)

MONA: MONDAY AT TEN ... CALLED MY COMPOSER
           THURSDAY AT SIX ... FOUND MY COMPOSER

(FELICIA enters wearing a Pucci mini; sunglasses on her forehead á là Gina Lollobrigida.)

FELICIA: FRIDAY AT THREE ... YES, I'LL BE THERE TO
           PLAY!

MONA: *(Admonishing FELICIA to be on time)* FRIDAY AT
           FOUR!

FELICIA: FRIDAY AT FOUR
           GOD, HOW I WISH I HAD ONE MORE DAY!

(LUCY, BOBBY, and CHARLEY enter: LUCY in bell-bottom jeans and a peasant blouse; BOBBY in a ponytail, tie-dye; CHARLEY, as always, the Yalie, wearing "preppy" sports jacket and tie.)

THE CLASS: MUSICAL COMEDY
                MUSICAL COMEDY CLASS
                WRITE A GOOD SONG ...
                HONEY, YOU PASS!

MONA: *(To Ed)* Loved your song last week.

ED: I haven't presented a song yet.

MONA: What was I thinking of?

ED: You were thinking of your song.

ALL: WEDNESDAY AT NINE...

BOBBY: SENSUAL PLEASURE

ALL: THURSDAY AT NINE...

LUCY: PERIODONTIST

ALL: FRIDAY AT NINE...

ED: OFFICE, BUT NOT FOR LONG!

ED & THE CLASS:
                FRIDAY AT FOUR FRIDAY AT FOUR

MEN: GATHER THE CLAN

WOMEN: BEES TO THE HIVE

MEN: PALPABLY,

WOMEN: TANGIBLY,

COMPANY: BRIEFLY ALIVE AS

FELICIA, BOBBY & LUCY:
        I GET TO TRY MY

MONA, ED & CHARLEY:
        I GET TO TRY MY

ED & THE CLASS:
        I GET TO TRY MY...
        SONG!

(By the end of the number, the group has brought in chairs that establish LEHMAN'*s classroom, and we are immediately in mid-class, with* BOBBY *playing the piano, presenting a new song, and* LEHMAN *presiding over the class. A sign-up sheet sits prominently on the piano.)*

BOBBY: LET'S FUCK
           BUT WE'LL CALL IT "MATING"
           LET'S FUCK
           BUT WE'LL CALL IT "BLISS"

           DO TEN UNSPEAKABLE THINGS TO ME
           HARD AND OFTEN
           CALL THAT "HEY, LET'S KISS!"

*(*BOBBY, *thrilled with his own work, looks to the class for the compliments he knows he's to receive. There is dead silence in the room.)*

LEHMAN: And Helen Keller sings this ... where?

BOBBY: The Act I Finale: the first time she makes love—it's amazing, but Helen was really a very passionate woman.

LEHMAN: And you feel that this is material for a musical?

BOBBY: It's never been done before. I mean, it's really hard to find a good story, with romance, and, you know, sexy stuff.

LEHMAN: Thank you, Bobby. Having conducted and arranged over a hundred Broadway shows, sometimes I think I've heard everything. How wrong I am.

BOBBY: *(reading Lehman's words as praise)* Well, you asked for a charm song and this is what came out.

(BOBBY takes his seat.)

LEHMAN: Remarkable!

BOBBY: Next week I'm going to prove to you that I can make Helen Keller's "Waa-Waa" song work as a rock number.

LEHMAN: Bobby, I'm sure rock music has its place—*(Pointing as far away as he can, with great distaste)*—somewhere...

(ED tries, as inconspicuously as possible, to get to the sign-up sheet without being noticed. LEHMAN notices.)

LEHMAN: Mr. Kleban, what in the key of F are you doing?

(All look at ED)

ED: —Taking my name off the sign-up sheet.

LEHMAN: It speaks! You've been taking your name off the sign-up sheet every class for the last 13 weeks.

ED: Well, it's just that I don't really think I'm really ready to present. Yet.

LEHMAN: Think again. You've been coming for weeks trying to squirm out of playing a song and today's the day.

ED: Right. Okay. It's just that you asked us to write a charm song for today and I'm not completely sure I understand.

LEHMAN: Why's that?

ED: Well last week, you said that a charm song—*(looking at his notes)* "has an optimistic feeling with a steadier sense of movement than one finds in most ballads."

LEHMAN: Correct.

ED: But I thought in a modern musical, all the songs have to either advance the plot—or illuminate character—

LEHMAN: It's like this, Mr. Kleban. Charm songs give the audience a break from worrying if Eliza Doolittle's gonna learn proper English.

CHARLEY: Or if the Farmer and the Cowman should be friends.

LEHMAN: Yes.

FELICIA: Or who's going to succeed in business—

LEHMAN: Right. A charm song is the southern belle of musicals—it don't have to do a lick of work—it just makes the audience smile.

ED: But that's so unspecific. I mean, if you ask me to write a song about a guy sitting at the bar at the Beverly Hills Hotel having just ordered two martinis on the day his wife of twenty years has run off with their Filipino gardener—that I can do. But a song to make the audience "smile." There's nothing to hold onto. That's hard.

LEHMAN: Don't look so serious, Mr. Kleban. Think "Put On a Happy Face."

(Musical intro: "Charm Song")

LUCY: "Once in Love With Amy."

LEHMAN: Right.

FELICIA: "Standin' on the Corner."

LEHMAN: Right.

BOBBY: "Poor Judd Is Dead."

LEHMAN: Wrong.

ED: Mr. Engel, I understand the idea. But are they necessary?

LEHMAN: *(Thinking: are you kidding?)* Mr. Kleban—
           CHARM SONG
           NOTHIN' TO IT
           CHARM SONG
           YOU COULD DO IT
           TAKE A LESSON FROM THE KID
           YOU'LL BE AWF'LY GLAD YOU DID

           CHARM SONG
           BLITHE AND BREEZY
           CHARM SONG
           LOOKS SO EASY
           IF YOU WANNA GET AHEAD
           IT'S THE WAY TO KNOCK 'EM DEAD

           THEY DON'T REALLY HAFTA LAUGH OUT
               LOUD

THE CLASS: *(HA-HA-HA!)*

LEHMAN: DO THAT CHARM SONG AND TOMORROW AT
          TEN,
          THERE'LL BE A CROWD
          TO HEAR YOUR

LEHMAN & THE CLASS:
          CHARM SONG

LEHMAN: SELL THOSE TICKETS

LEHMAN & THE CLASS:
          CHARM SONG

LEHMAN: STICKY WICKETS
          MELT AWAY
          IT NEVER DO NO HARM
          TO TURN THEIR HEADS
          TURN ON THE

LEHMAN & THE CLASS:
          CHARRRRRRRRM!

ED: How would you write a charm song for a musical
          about Fred Astaire?

LEHMAN: *(after a beat)* ... Gingerly!

MONA: How would you write a charm song for a musical
          about the Flying Wallendas?

LEHMAN: I'd try it in swing time.

   (The CLASS groans)

LEHMAN: YOU'RE IN BOSTON WITH A SLOW ACT ONE
          CUT THAT BALLAD AND THE SHOW WILL
          RUN ON SIMPLY

LEHMAN & THE CLASS:
　　　　CHARM SONGS

LEHMAN: SHORT AND SNAPPY

THE CLASS: CHARM SONGS

LEHMAN: KEEP 'EM HAPPY
　　　　SHOOT THAT SMILE
　　　　I SWEAR YOU CAN'T GO WRONG

LEHMAN: SO LIVE AND LEARN
　　　　DO A GOOD TURN
　　　　IT ALWAYS GOES
　　　　IT SAVES MOST SHOWS

THE CLASS: *(at same time as above)*
　　　　UMM-HMM
　　　　AHH-HAH
　　　　IT ALWAYS GOES
　　　　ED
　　　　IT DO, IT DO!

　　(All look at ED *)*

LEHMAN: 'CAUSE WHEN THEY HEAD FOR SARDI'S
　　　　WHISTLING RIGHT ALONG . . .
　　　　THEY'LL TURN AND SAY
　　　　"WHAT WAS THAT CHARM . . . ING . . .
　　　　SONNNNNNNNNG?"

　　　　I WOULDN'T KID YA!

　　　　So. Mr. Kleban? Clear?

ED:　　　Crystal.

LEHMAN: Good. You're on.

ED: Me? Oh, no, no, no. My song needs a total rewrite.
           Total.

LEHMAN: Mr. Kleban—

ED: I don't know about anyone else, but I'd love to hear
           Charley's song.

CHARLEY: Good idea. *(He rises)*

LEHMAN: Charley, sit.

   (CHARLEY *sits*)

           Front and center, Kleban.

ED: The thing is, it's a kinda long song, and I'm not sure
           there's even time to—

LEHMAN: No play-ee, no stayee. Hit it!

ED: *(Mustering his courage decisively)* Fine.

   (He stands up and gathers his paraphernalia)

LEHMAN: Okay, kiddies. Remember your own first time—a
           little empathy.

FELICIA: Why?

ED: Sorry, but is there any way to turn down the heat?

LUCY: I'll open a window.

ED: NO! Draft! Maybe open the door. Not all the way!—
           Just a crack—

(LUCY *adjusts the door and* ED *sets up at the piano: He places a pillow down on the piano bench, and, on top of the piano, lines up his electric pencil-sharpener, pencils,|pad, and his ashtray.*)

ED: Picture the world's greatest art gallery. The "Mona Lisa." Michelangelo's "David." Gauguin's famous paintings of Tahiti. Enter Harold, a college student who is having a kind of nervous breakdown. Harold's friends, worried about him, find him in the gallery, mesmerized by a Chagall painting of Paris. Knowing he loves to play jazz, they convince him to come to Europe with their band.

(He holds up pieces of paper for the lead-in to the song)

         Oh, there are a couple of lines, I wonder if you'd read them where indicated. Enter, Bob—

(CHARLEY *raises his hand.*)

CHARLEY: I'm Bob. *(Takes a "side")*

ED: —carrying a trumpet. And Dick—

BOBBY: Yo—*(Takes a "side")*

ED: —carrying a bass. You start, Charley.

CHARLEY (BOB):
         Right. Playing "Bob"—carrying a trumpet. *(As "Bob," reading the line badly)* "It'll be a great summer."

BOBBY (DICK):
         (As "Dick," even worse than CHARLEY*)* "Our band will play Gershwin all over Europe."

ED: Well. There's Harold, 19, in the middle of a crack-up, probably dying of—*(hypochondriacally touching the glands on his own neck, with some alarm)*—swollen glands—it may be his last summer on earth. What's he got to lose? So he packs his lead sheets, three drip-dry shirts, polyester slacks his mother bought at S. Klein's, and they're off.

FELICIA: We're in for it now—

ED (HAROLD):
    BOB AT THE WHEEL OF A RENTED CAR
    DICK MUNCHING CRACKERS AND BRIE
    AND PARIS THROUGH THE WINDOW
    PARIS THROUGH THE WINDOW . . .
    THEM, IT, ME . . .

(The class disappears for the duration of the number. LIGHT CHANGE. Three rolling classroom-chairs become a cramped automobile, and a slide of Chagall's painting, "Paris Through the Window" becomes the backdrop for the scene as ED *relives his first trip to Europe.)*

ED: DRIVING FROM BRUSSELS, WE TRAVELED ALL
        NIGHT
    TIRED . . . CRANKY . . . FIGHTING
    CRAMPED IN OUR CAR, WHEN WE SLEPT ALL
        OUR DREAMS WERE OF HOME
    BOB DID THE DRIVING AND I READ THE MAP
    FINALLY, I FELL ASLEEP
    NEXT THING I HEARD WAS FROM DICK IN
        THE BACK

BOBBY (DICK):
    "GUESS WHERE? . . . CREEP!"

ED (HAROLD):
    PARIS THROUGH THE WINDOW...

CHARLEY (BOB):
    GARBAGE

ED (HAROLD):
> PARIS THROUGH THE WINDOW...

BOBBY (DICK):
> RAIN

ED (HAROLD):
> PARIS THROUGH THE WINDOW... SEVEN...
> MORNING... PARIS!!!
> BOB SAID,

CHARLEY (BOB):
> "IT'S FILTHY,"

ED (HAROLD):
> AND DICK SAID,

BOBBY (DICK):
> "IT SMELLS"

ED (HAROLD):
> BUT IF I SAID A THING IT WAS, "WHERE?"
> EIGHTEEN YEARS OLD, AND BETWEEN ME
> AND PARIS WAS GLASS AND AIR

ALL: PARIS WITH THE WINDOW OPEN
> PARIS WITH THE WINDOW WIDE
> PARIS WITH THE WINDOW OPEN

ED (HAROLD):
> AND WITH ME, HANGING OUTSIDE!

BOBBY (DICK):
> "IS THIS THE PARIS,"

ED (HAROLD):
> DICK SHOUTED IN FRENCH,

BOBBY (DICK):
"THAT THE POETS HAVE SUNG TO EXCESS?"

ED (HAROLD):
AND I JUST WHISPERED "YES"

ALL: YES ...

CHARLEY (BOB):
PARIS FROM MY TENTH-GRADE TEXTBOOK

BOBBY (DICK):
PARIS WITH MY LOUSY FRENCH

ED (HAROLD):
PARIS WITH THE TWISTY ...
(OH, YOU KNOW THAT ...)

ALL: PARIS!!!

ED (HAROLD):
TURNING ONE CORNER I ALMOST FELL OUT
WHEN MY KNEE HIT THE LOCK ON THE DOOR

CHARLEY (BOB) & BOBBY (DICK):
USING GOOD JUDGMENT WAS NEVER WHAT
PARIS WAS FAMOUS FOR

BOBBY (DICK):
PARIS ON THE EIGHTEENTH AUGUST

CHARLEY (BOB):
PARIS WITH THE GARBAGE ...

ED (HAROLD):
... FINE!

ALL: PARIS THROUGH THE WINDOW ...

ED (HAROLD):
> AND THEY MISSED IT
> THAT PARIS WAS MINE
> NOTHING THAT HAPPENED AND NOTHING
>   WE SAW
> IN THE WEEK THAT WE STAYED COULD
>   COMPARE
> TO SIMPLY BEING THERE

(BOB and DICK *fade into the past.)*

ED (HAROLD):
> AND BOB WENT ON TO A WALL STREET JOB
> AND DICK TO A LAW SCHOOL DEGREE
> BUT PARIS THROUGH THE WINDOW
> PARIS THROUGH THE WINDOW
> STAYED WITH ME ...

(LIGHTS indicate we are back in the class. The CLASS *is silent.)*

LEHMAN: Well. There. Class: Critique.

ED: Wait—(ED *sharpens his pencil)*

LEHMAN: Someone ... Anyone ... Mona?

MONA: *(Baffled)* It was ...

ED: *(Intensely interested, pencil poised)* Yes?

MONA: Interesting.

ED: *(Writing)* Interesting.

CHARLEY: I gotta say, there are some really very—uh, fine moments, notions in the piece—but truthfully— "Paris." I mean, "April in Paris," "The Last Time I Saw Paris"—Do we need another Paris song?

BOBBY: How about Helsinki?

ED: Excuse me?

BOBBY: "Helsinki through the window ... "

ED: I don't think—you see, the point is ...

LUCY: *(Clearly impressed)* It's not like anything I've ever heard.

ED: But is that good or bad?

FELICIA: But is it an opening number, a ballad, a charm song—just what is it?

(THE CLASS *all speak at once, passionately arguing over the merit of Ed's song. Defeated,* ED *begins packing up his stuff.*)

LEHMAN: Enough! Original is what it is. It's a wonderfully crafted, truthful song. I have high expectations of you, Mr. Kleban.

ED: "High expectations." Thank you. *(To the class)* And thank you for your notes.

LEHMAN: All right, class, please remember your assignment for next week is to write a charm song for a scene from *Streetcar Named Desire*. And, please, kiddies, spare me yet another ditty titled "The Kindness of Strangers." *(Leaving, his traditional salutation)* Abyssinia!

(LEHMAN *exits.* THE CLASS *packs up their stuff*)

BOBBY: Frankfort.

ED: Excuse me?

BOBBY: "Frankfort Through the Window."

ED: Oh, thanks.

BOBBY: *(Introducing himself)* Bobby del Vecchio.

ED: Ed Kleban—

BOBBY: —and if you ever need a drummer, my backbeat is genius.

ED: Thanks, I'll remember that.

(BOBBY exits. LUCY comes over to ED)

LUCY: Welcome to the club. Hi, I'm Lucy Chaplin, I sit way in the back. Your "Paris" song—wow—

ED: You really liked it?

LUCY: I'd love to do one of your songs for an audition sometime.

ED: I haven't written that many. Songs. Yet. But I write every day. So, you sing on Broadway, huh?

LUCY: You know in *Mame,* when Angela Lansbury does those high kicks as she walks down center singing the title number?

ED: Sure.

LUCY: Do you remember the third redhead from her left?

ED: *(Way impressed)* You know, I think I do.

LUCY: Well, I'm behind her.

ED: Cool! You know you're the first person I've ever met
             who was actually in a Broadway show.

LUCY: And you're the first person I've ever met who may
             actually write one.

ED: Really?

LUCY: Really.

ED: I'm trying hard not to have a dopey smile on my face
             or throw up all over you or something. I mean my
             girlfriend, Sophie, likes my songs—but ...

  (FELICIA *sidles up to them*)

FELICIA: Lehman likes to encourage beginners. Felicia de la
             Luz Flores. Last year's Cole Porter fellow. I work at
             Columbia Records, too.

ED: Never seen you there.

FELICIA: On the twenty-third floor—

ED: That explains it.

FELICIA: Come by my cubicle, we'll shoot the breeze, I've got
             some thoughts.

ED: Oh boy. (FELICIA *moves away as* CHARLEY
             approaches)

CHARLEY: Kleban, a couple of notes: Going into the bridge you
             might try a diminished chord before the key change.
             Or an augmented 7th. And check your transition into
             the coda, I'd voice that B flat chord just a bit differ-
             ently.

ED: Thanks. I'll absolutely look at it.

CHARLEY: Do.

(CHARLEY *joins* FELICIA *on the sidelines.*)

LUCY: See you next week? And your smile's not dopey.

(LUCY *meets up with* CHARLEY *and* FELICIA *by the exit.*)

He's cute. And he's good, too.

FELICIA: *(To* CHARLEY *)* Whatdya think?

CHARLEY: He's so good, I hope he has deep psychological prob-
             lems.

ED: *(A bit panicked)* Oh, m'God, did anyone see my ther-
             mometer?

FELICIA: *(Observing Ed)* Bingo.

(MUSICAL GLISS/LIGHT CHANGE)

MEMORIAL LIMBO, 1988

*(*BOBBY *stands in the golden memorial light. He holds index
cards with notes for his speech.* ED, *as earlier, the ghost at his own
Memorial, stands on the sidelines listening in, unseen by* BOBBY.*)*

BOBBY: Picture Ed: The world's greatest Mets fan.

ED: Come on, Bobby, there's more to life than a song.
             Sports. Girls. That's it.

BOBBY: The 1969 World Series—

ED: The Mets against the Orioles! Tell it right, Bobby.

BOBBY: Ed and me in the bleachers at Shea Stadium. Don
           Clendennon cracks this home run into the stands.

ED: Right at me.

BOBBY: Ed ducks. I catch the ball.

ED: Right!

BOBBY: I knew how much it meant to him. I tried to give it to
           him—but he wouldn't take it. He just kept going on
           about my courage.

ED: A true fact.

BOBBY: But to me, Ed was the one with courage.

ED: What!?

BOBBY: The miracle isn't that he wrote so little, but that he
           wrote so much. And with all his inner ... stuffings, I
           knew what it took for him to expose to the world, for
           the few moments it takes to hear a song, the real Ed.
           Now that's courage.

ED: Bobby!

BOBBY: I loved the guy.

ED: Back at ya, pal. You are a true friend.

BOBBY: There was one thing I could never figure out—

ED: Oh, what's that?

BOBBY: He was such a nebbish—what did all the women see
           in him?

ED: WHAT!

(MUSICAL GLISS/LIGHT CHANGE)

SCENE 5

LIMBO (MONA), 1967

MONA: *(She has found his thermometer and dangles it seduc-*
            tively) Edward . . .

(ED—still speaking to us as the ghost at his memorial—stands in
front of MONA trying to block her from view.)

ED (THE GHOST):
            Oh, no, don't watch this. It's—uh—private.

MONA: You dropped your thermometer.

(Mona's seductiveness draws ED back to his youth in 1967.
He responds to MONA)

ED (IN HIS TWENTIES):
            Thanks.

(It is clear he is smitten. The ghost of ED, embarrassed, takes a
beat, then, trying to cover up, turns to the audience)

ED (THE GHOST):
            Okay. I know I said "truth." But—let's go back to my
            childhood in the Bronx.

MONA: (Continuing to play up to YOUNG ED) I thought we
            might get together after class.

ED (THE GHOST):
>   Third-grade school play: I was Davy Crockett and
>   right in the middle of my big song, I broke out in this
>   weird horizontal rash—

MONA: We should get to know each other.

ED (THE GHOST):
>   The kids started to laugh, so my mother rushed on
>   stage and finished singing the song.

MONA: I have this feeling we'd be good together ...

ED (THE GHOST):
>   —In a coonskin cap.

MONA: Edward ...

ED (THE GHOST):
>   I'm not saying it was seminal—but Dr. Nodine sug-
>   gested that I consider why I—

SOPHIE: *(appearing in* LIMBO *)* The truth, Eddie!

(ED, *forcing himself to be truthful, turns to* MONA, *and relives
what happened in 1967.*)

ED (IN HIS TWENTIES):
>   ... Whatdyasay?

(SOPHIE *exits.*)

MONA: I have this feeling we'd be good together.

ED: At what? *(He thinks)* Oh, thanks, I'm flattered, really,
>   but I write both music and lyrics ...

(as she moves closer)

MONA: I mean in bed.

ED: ... and music.

MONA: I really dig songwriters.

ED: Songwriters? I never thought of that.

MONA: Talent really turns me on.

ED: Really? But I have a girlfriend.

MONA: *(Thwarted)* Too bad for me ...

ED: She's in Philadelphia.

MONA: *(She brightens up)* Too bad for her ...

ED: But I suppose there's no harm in discussing the subtleties of interior rhyme.

MONA: It's a territory I need to explore.

          YOU ARE NOW ENTERING MONA
          POPULATION: TWO
          DANGEROUS CURVES
          SOFT SHOULDERS
          MONA WELCOMES YOU!
          DRIVING THROUGH MONA
          YIELDING IN MONA
          PARKING AND SPENDING THE DAY
          MODERN AND LOVELY
          WELL WORTH A DETOUR
          MONA INVITES YOU TO STAY!

(LIGHTS UP on SOPHIE *in* LIMBO*)*

SOPHIE: Can't wait for you to come to Philadelphia this weekend!

ED: I'm writing my "I Want" song. I may have ...

MONA & ED:
              TO STAY ...

(LIGHTS OUT on SOPHIE *in* LIMBO. ED *and* MONA *share a romantic moment.)*

ED: Oh, Mona, you are so amazing—! But I want you to
              know—early morning's my best writing time, so
              you'll have to leave the apartment by 5 A.M. And if we
              ever go back to your apartment, you'll have to get rid
              of those cats ...

(MONA *pushes* ED *away)*

MONA: YOU ARE NOW LEAVING MONA
              POPULATION: ONE
              WATCH POSTED SIGNS
              DRIVE SAFELY
              LIFE CAN BE FUN ...

(ED *pulls* MONA *back, giving her a slow, long, passionate kiss.)*

              You're a fast learner. See you next week.

              AVOID DEAD ENDS AND CUL-DE-SACS
              AND HURRY, HURRY, HURRY, HURRY, HURRY,
              HURRY, HURRY, HURRY BACK
              HURRY BACK

(SOPHIE *walks in unexpectedly, carrying a gift)*

SOPHIE: Surprise!

MONA: HURRY BACK!

(MONA *exits)*

SOPHIE: So she's the "I Want" song you were working on—well I want out.

ED: One little indiscretion.

SOPHIE: So that means it doesn't count?

ED: She didn't mean anything. She just dug my songs.

SOPHIE: And you dug her. You can't switch women like you change keys.

ED: She was there. And, goddammit, you weren't.

SOPHIE: You're making this MY fault?

ED: I need you. You know that.

SOPHIE: And what about what I need? You have no idea who I am.

ED: Of course I do. You're going to be a doctor! Blood clots, intestines, secretions . . . Jeez, I'm getting a little clammy here . . .

SOPHIE: Good.

ED: Hey, let me play you this song I just wrote.

SOPHIE: For her? (*She moves closer to the door as* ED *blocks her*)

ED: (*One final plea, no more games*) Sophie, wait. Please. Please, don't go. I need you.

SOPHIE: Not anymore. The truth is you just need an audience.

ED: Don't you ever say that to me again.

SOPHIE: You needn't worry about that. *(SOPHIE throws down the keys and exits)*

ED: *(Calling out the door after her . . .)* SOPHIE!

(We begin to make out ED's friends in a half-lit LIMBO. DR. NODINE quietly enters and slowly walks towards ED, as if to take him back to the hospital)

FELICIA: His life was a bust.

LEHMAN: Wasted his potential.

BOBBY: Couldn't cope with success.

MONA: Not marriage material.

COMPANY: *(Variously)* SOPHIE WAS RIGHT!

ED: *(Shutting out all the voices in his head and stopping NODINE from getting any closer)* No!

  (DR. NODINE stops in his tracks)

ED: Okay. New song. Harold's childhood sweetheart leaves him.

(ED begins to play the vamp of "Under Separate Cover." All including NODINE exit, and the stage goes black except for ED and his piano in a tight spot, vamp still playing, ever more urgently, as if the sheer ferocity of it could obliterate the pain. He rethinks the song.)

           No, Harold cheats on his . . . wife. She throws him out. Alone, she writes him a letter. *(Writing on a yellow legal pad)* Under separate cover are the records and the books and the ashtray that you gave me in

November—*(Scratches it out—Tossing the legal pad)*
No. No ashtray. Sophie hates cigarettes.

(The light widens and we can make out LUCY *standing by* ED *with a piece of paper in her hand.* ED *continues to write as she sings.)*

LUCY: UNDER SEPARATE COVER
ARE TEN CARTONS AND A TRUNK
AND THE BICYCLE YOU HAD SENT HOME
FROM ENGLAND
AND THE SHIRTS YOUR MOTHER MEN-
TIONED ALTHOUGH
SOME OF THEM HAVE SHRUNK
AND SOME OLD ASSORTED JUNK

AND THE BEST PART OF MY LIFE
AS YOUR FIRST AND ONLY WIFE
AND THE FIRM BELIEF THAT LOVE HAS GONE
FOR GOOD

ED: But Harold's wife smokes. *(*ED *scribbles on his yellow pad . . . and* LUCY *continues)*

LUCY: UNDER SEPARATE COVER
ARE THE RECORDS AND THE BOOKS
AND THE ASHTRAY THAT I GAVE YOU IN
OCTOBER
AND THE HOPE THAT ALL THE NEIGHBORS
WILL STOP
SHOOTING ME THOSE LOOKS
THERE ARE FAR TOO MANY COOKS

AND THE BEST PART OF MY LIFE
AS YOUR FIRST AND ONLY WIFE
AND THE FIRM BELIEF THAT LOVE IS GONE
FOR GOOD

ED: I CAN HEAR THE MUSIC OF THE PHONO-
               GRAPH STILL
            I CAN HEAR THE MUSIC OF THE LAUGHTER
            I CAN HEAR THE MUSIC AND I'M SURE THAT I
               WILL
            HEAR IT EVER AFTER

LUCY & ED:
            HEAR IT EVER AFTER . . .

(SOPHIE *enters, with a suitcase*)

LUCY & SOPHIE:
            UNDER SEPARATE COVER
            ARE THE REMNANTS OF MY HEART

ED, LUCY & SOPHIE:
            AND THE WISH THAT YOU ARE FLOURISHING
               TOMORROW
            AND THE IRONCLAD CONVICTION WE'LL DO
               BETTER NOW APART
            AND THE TIME HAS COME TO START

LUCY & SOPHIE:
            AND THE BEST PART OF MY LIFE
            AS YOUR FIRST AND ONLY WIFE
            AND THE FIRM BELIEF THAT LOVE IS GONE . . .

ED: AND THE FIRM BELIEF THAT LOVE IS GONE . . .

ED, LUCY & SOPHIE (IN A ROUND):
            AND THE FIRM BELIEF THAT LOVE IS GONE . . .

ED, LUCY & SOPHIE:
            FOR GOOD . . .

(SOPHIE *takes one more look around and exits as electric sign flashing the word "RECORDING" lights up, and it becomes clear that* ED *and* LUCY *are in a recording studio. Behind them we now see a wall covered with Columbia Records album covers from the sixties: Janis Joplin, Dylan, Barbra Streisand, Simon and Garfunkel, Santana, Sondheim's* Company)

SCENE 6

A RECORDING STUDIO

AT COLUMBIA RECORDS, 1967-1971

(LUCY *remains near* ED *at the piano.*)

ENGINEER (VO):
　　　　　　Sounds good in there, Ed.

LUCY:　　　You miss her a lot, don't you?

ED:　　　　What?

LUCY:　　　Sophie.

ED:　　　　Sophie? It's just a song.

LUCY:　　　It's perfect.

ED:　　　　It's getting there.

LUCY:　　　It's meticulous. Not a false rhyme, a missed stress—

ED:　　　　It has to be. (ED *is silent*)

LUCY:　　　Why does it have to be?

ED: Because it can be. Are you all right?

(Despite herself, LUCY lets her emotions show.)

LUCY: Oh, I'm going through this stupid divorce thing. Don's a stage manager, and we're both on the road so much we barely see each other. The marriage was a cup of coffee. But your song—I mean, how'd you know? It was like you saw inside me ...

ED: *(Affectionately)* How about coming over for dinner tonight? I make a splendid roast chicken.

LUCY: Sounds good. But I like you too much to be on the rebound.

ED: It's just a chicken.

LUCY: Yeah. And that was just a song. Maybe some other time.

(FELICIA ENTERS, now wearing a sophisticated suit.)

FELICIA: Hey, guys.

ED: Felicia! What are you doing here?

FELICIA: Goddard Lieberson called me into his office. Offered to make me his private secretary.

LUCY: Impressive.

FELICIA: Puh-leese—so fifties. Do I look like Doris Day? I convinced Lieberson to make me the first woman executive at Columbia Records.

LUCY: Right on, Felicia!

The Company of *A Class Act*. All photographs by Joan Marcus of the 2001 Broadway production.

The Company

Lonny Price as Ed and Sara Ramirez as Felicia

The Company

ED: Great!

FELICIA: I love the music business!

(Coming aggressively closer to ED *as she speaks)*

What I hate is how the bigwigs on the 24th floor think I'm only working here until some lucky guy grabs me up and marries me.

ED: Don't look at me.

FELICIA: *(Looking right over his head)* I'm not. But from now on, you better get used to looking at me. I'm running your department.

ED: Oh, my God.

LUCY: *(To Ed)* Well, I have an audition. Thanks for letting me do the demo, Ed.

ED: *(To Lucy)* Don't leave me.

LUCY: 'Bye, Felicia.

*(*LUCY *exits)*

FELICIA: A demo?

ED: It's another song from my "Gallery" musical. It's about this guy Harold, and in this song he—

FELICIA: Wake up! Broadway's dead. Bob Dylan just went gold. "The times they are a-changin'," and I'm a-changin' with 'em. I'm quitting the workshop. I'm gonna be the first woman who owns her own label—

ED: And I'm gonna be the first person in the workshop who writes a Broadway musical.

FELICIA: They're dinosaurs!

ED: Next week I booked the studio to do a demo of four
            songs from my *Thousand Clowns* musical.

FELICIA: On company time? I don't think so.

            A TINY LIBERTY, BUT MISTER, EVEN SO
            YOU KNOW WHAT EENY SAID TO MEENY-
                MINEY-MO
            DON'T DO IT
            DON'T DO IT AGAIN

ED: A couple of producers are interested in the show.

FELICIA: They're dinosaurs!
            YOU TAKE ADVANTAGE ON THE SLIMMEST OF
                PRETEXT
            IF I SHOULD LET YOU WHO'S TO SAY WHAT
                MIGHT BE NEXT?
            DON'T DO IT
            DON'T DO IT AGAIN

ED: Okay. Fine, I'll just record the best two.

FELICIA: DON'T DO IT AGAIN!
            BANISH THE THOUGHT
            PUT IT RIGHT OUT OF YOUR MIND
            TEDDY BEAR, EDDIE BEAR
            LEAVE THE HONEY BEHIND

    (Gesturing toward the rock album covers)

            Look! The Future! Simon and Garfunkel! Santana!

ED: *(Gesturing toward the* Company *album cover)*
            Sondheim!

FELICIA: Who?

ED: *(horrified)* Felicia!

FELICIA: OUR LITTLE MEETING HAS AN AIR OF LIVE
AND LET
AND IN YOUR ROOM TONIGHT YOU'LL
PROBABLY FORGET
DON'T DO IT
DON'T DO IT AGAIN

Oh, and Ed, you better keep your schedule open. I've got meetings planned evenings and weekends for the next two months.

ED: No way, Felicia. Evenings and weekends are the only time I get to write.

FELICIA: *(not listening)* And Ed, you better forget the workshop.

ED: Never. The workshop means everything to me.

FELICIA: Except a paycheck.

ED: Felicia, you're pushing it!
THOUGH YOUR ARRIVAL IS THIS MORNING'S
HOTTEST NEWS
YOU THINK YOU'LL MOVE ME INTO
ANYTHING YOU CHOOSE?
DON'T DO IT
DON'T DO IT AGAIN!

FELICIA: Friday—record convention in Dallas.

ED: Friday—I'm playing my *Scaramouche* musical in class.

FELICIA: Friday, Dallas.

ED: Saturday, Dallas.

FELICIA: Monday—dinner with Cy Coleman.

ED: Lunch with Cy!

FELICIA: Now you're pushing it!

FELICIA & ED:
            DON'T DO IT
            THEN COUNT TO TEN
            THEN . . .

FELICIA: *(Sings a high note she knows he can't hit)* DON'T
            DO IT!

ED: *(Hitting it)* DON'T DO IT AGAIN!

FELICIA: AND AGAIN!

ED: AND AGAIN!

FELICIA: AND AGAIN!

ED: AND AGAIN!

FELICIA: AND AGAIN!

ED AND FELICIA:
            AND AGAIN, AND AGAIN
            AND AGAIN, AND AGAIN, AND AGAIN!

FELICIA: Do we understand each other?

ED: Perfectly.

ED AND FELICIA:
>YEAH!

FELICIA: *(Checking her schedule)* Good. Tomorrow, Barbra—

ED: *(enthused)*—Streisand?

FELICIA: Right.

ED: Well, now there's something I wouldn't mind pro—

FELICIA: *(checking her notes)* Uh-uh. Mike Berniker down the hall. Your next assignment is Andrey Voznesensky reading his poetry in Russian.

ED: Shoot me.

FELICIA: And don't forget, Ed, dinner tonight at the Four Seasons. I promised Percy Faith we'd discuss Schoenberg's *Verklärte Nacht.*

ED: Are you trying to kill me?

FELICIA: Tuesday, Dorothy Parker—

ED: No dinner—

FELICIA: Okay, forget dinner. With her, liquor is quicker. Wednesday night—

ED: Wednesday evening I'm working on a Gauguin song for my "Gallery" musical. It's fascinating. He started out as this rich banker in Paris and he gave it all up to paint in Tahiti...

FELICIA: —where he died of syphilis. If you insist on writing these musicals that no one will ever see, at least let's not talk about them. Now, schedule the recording session, do the mix, write the liner notes, stick to the budget, plan the jacket covers, come in on deadline and...

(MUSICAL STING as FELICIA *freezes and the lights on her go to half)*

ED: *(Musing. His inner thoughts)*
           WERE I IN GAUGUIN'S SHOES
           WHAT WOULD I HAVE TO LOSE?
           I WOULD EMBRACE THE MUSE
           AND EVEN THANK HER

(LIGHTS UP FULL on FELICIA*)*

FELICIA: Percy Faith went gold! You get a Diner's Card and the bilingual Jim Nabors album: "Je m'appelle Jim." Schedule the recording session, do the mix, write the liner notes, stick to the budget, plan the jacket cover, come in on deadline, isn't this fun?

*(*FELICIA *freezes. LIGHT CHANGE)*

ED: AND I WOULD CHOOSE
           WHATEVER GAUGUIN CHOSE
           AND WALK AROUND IN ONLY GAUGUIN'S
              CLOTHES
           AND I WOULD GO WHEREVER GAUGUIN
           GOES HE WAS A BANKER.

(LIGHTS UP on FELICIA*)*

FELICIA: Jim Nabors loves you! You get a bonus—the Jim Nabors Christmas album: "Jim Live at the Vatican"! Now, schedule the recording session, do the mix, write the liner notes, stick to the budget, plan the jacket cover, come in on deadline...

(FELICIA *exits, still talking.*)

ED: AND AS HE SAT IN HIS CAGE
              LISTENING TO THE TAKEOVER BIDS
              (A HUNDRED AND TWO,
              A HUNDRED AND THREE)
              HE JUST FLEW INTO A RAGE
              AND SUDDENLY LEFT HIS WIFE AND HIS KIDS
              (DING–DONG!)
              FOR TROUBLE IN TAHITI
              (WASN'T HE A SWEETIE?)

              HAD I BUT GAUGUIN'S DASH
              HAD I HIS CUTE MOUSTACHE
              WHY I'D CONVERT TO CASH
              AND HAVE A BALL
              IF I WERE BANKER . . . PAINTER . . .
              GAUGUIN . . . COMMA! PAUL

(*LIGHT CHANGE: The backdrop is washed in a series of intense Gauguin colors which change from orange to blue to rose to green through the following sequence as* MONA *and* LUCY *ENTER in* ED'S *fantasy. They are dressed in all-white versions of their memorial costumes, which take on Gauguin colors as the lights change*)

MONA & LUCY: FABULOUS FEET
              INDESCRIBABLY SWEET
              IN DISTRESS IN DA STREET
              GOIN' HIPPITTY-HOPPITTY
              HANSEL AND GRETEL
              JUMPED OVER THE SHTETEL
              BUT OH, THOSE SILLIES!
              TAGGIN' ALONG
              AGAGGA-LING
              THRONG OF CUTIES
              IN BOOTIES AND SUCH

ED: FETISH IS FINE
           (GOD KNOWS I HAVE MINE)
           BUT THIS IS A LITTLE TOO MUCH

MONA & LUCY:
           HEELING AND TOEING
           AND NONE OF THEM KNOWING
           THAT MY HEART IS GOING
           A-CLIPPITTY-CLOPPITY
           TAPPERS 'N SQUEAKERS
           OR FLAPPERS IN SNEAKERS
           I GET THE WILLIES!

ED: NEEDLESS TO SAY
           ANOTHER DAY

MONA & LUCY:
           AND SOMEBODY LOSES HIS GRIP . . .

ED: ME!

MONA & LUCY:
           A-TIPPITTY-TAP
           A-TIPPITTY-TAP
           A-TAPPITTY-TIP!

(CHARLEY & BOBBY ENTER in all-white versions of their
memorial costumes.)

CHARLEY, ED, BOBBY: (at same time as opposite page)
           WERE I IN
           GAUGUIN'S SHOES

           WHAT WOULD I HAVE TO LOSE?
           I WOULD EMBRACE THE MUSE

           AND EVEN THANK HER!
           AND I WOULD CHOOSE

WHATEVER GAUGUIN CHOSE

AND WALK AROUND
IN ONLY

GAUGUIN'S CLOTHES

AND I WOULD GO
WHEREVER GAUGUIN GOES

HE WAS A
BANKER

AND AS HE SAT IN HIS SOCKS
THINKIN' ABOUT THE MESS
HE WAS IN

HE SAID
"TO HELL WITH THE STOCKS!"
AND SUDDENLY THOUGHT OF ANTHONY
    QUINN

MONA, LUCY: (at same time as previous page)
    FABULOUS FEET INDESCRIBABLY SWEET
    IN DISTRESS IN DA STREET
    GOIN' HIPPITTY-HOPPITTY
    HANSEL AND GRETEL
    JUMPED OVER THE SHTETEL
    BUT OH THOSE SILLIES!
    TAGGIN' ALONG
    AGAGGA-LING THRONG OF CUTIES
    IN BOOTIES AND SUCH
    FETISH IS FINE
    (GOD KNOWS I HAVE MINE)
    BUT THIS IS A LITTLE TOO MUCH
    HEELING AND TOEING
    AND NONE OF THEM KNOWING
    THAT MY HEART IS

GOING
A-CLIPPITTY-CLOPPITTY
TAPPERS 'N SQUEAKERS
OR FLAPPERS IN SNEAKERS

I GET THE WILLIES!
NEEDLESS TO SAY
ANOTHER DAY
AND SOMEBODY LOSES HIS GRIP . . .

A-TIPPITTY-TAP,
A-TIPPITTY-TAP
A-TAPPITTY-TIP

YOU'RE ASKING
DO WE LOVE FEET?
YES WE DO
WE CANNOT TELL A LIE!
ABSENCE OF FEET

MAKES US BLUE
AND . . .

ALL: DING-DONG, DING-DONG!

(FELICIA *ENTERS in a Santa Claus hat, holding a Tiffany box*)

FELICIA: Double your salary! Expense account! Trips to our
           London office! When I own my own label, you'll be
           my Goddard Lieberson!!

ED: On, no! Now I'll never get out!

(ED *gestures to the conductor for the big finish of* HIS *fantasy.*)

           HAD I BUT . . .

ED WITH MONA & LUCY: MEN:
   GAUGUIN'S DASH   HIS DASH!
   HAD I BUT GAUGUIN'S PASH HIS PASH!
   HAD I BUT GAUGUIN'S STASH HIS STASH!
   I'D HAVE A BALL!   I'D HAVE A BALL!

   (Dance Break)

ALL: IF I WERE
           BANKER
           PAINTER
           GAUGUIN
           (FABULOUS FEET!)

MEN: PAUL!

WOMEN *(at same time)*:
           PAWWAWAWAWAWAWAWL!

ALL: CAUGHT IN A GRAB IN A GABBLE OF
               FABULOUS FEET
           PAUL!
              (Big playoff encore:)

           IF I WERE
           BANKER
           PAINTER
           GAUGUIN
           (FABULOUS FEET!)

MEN: PAUL!

WOMEN *(at same time)*:
           PAWWAWAWAWAWAWAWL!

ALL: CAUGHT IN A GRAB IN A GABBLE OF
               FABULOUS FEET
           PAUL!

(The COMPANY *exits, but* ED *remains on stage, as a LIGHT CHANGE brings us back to the reality of Columbia Records.)*

SCENE 7

COLUMBIA RECORDS, 1972

(LEHMAN *enters.)*

LEHMAN: Ed—so how was the flight from London?

ED: Seconal is a wonderful drug. Never again.

LEHMAN: Well, you missed Charley's opening! That song he wrote for the musical revue got a rave in the *Village Voice*! I tell you, Charley's floating on air!

ED: Charley floating?

LEHMAN: Now that he has a foot in the door, he's getting offers to write music for television, movies, possibly an off-Broadway show...

   (ED turns away)

   Ed, are you all right?

ED: No, no, I'm fine. You see I'm not like the others in class. I don't get jealous—*(losing it)* IT'S NOT IN MY NATURE!

LEHMAN: Ed—

ED: Oh, Lehman, I write song after song, show after show, just a bunch of tapes piling up in my closet.

LEHMAN: Ed—listen to me—

ED: I know, you always told me it wasn't going to be easy. But Lehman, I'm not like other people. I don't know if you've noticed—I'm a little peculiar.

LEHMAN: Really?

ED: *(Hiding his stay in the mental hospital)* I just don't know if I can keep going on like this. *("Fountain in the Garden" music underscores...)* There's something about me that I never tell anyone. Something I just can't talk about.

LEHMAN: And I'll never ask. If you'll never ask what it was like to grow up Jewish and a sissy in Mississippi. A Mississippi sissy. How many s's are there in "Mississippi Sissy?" I left my Southern accent on the train to New York, and found a new life conducting on Broadway, where I fit in among all the wonderful oddballs. So don't ever ask about all that.

ED: I never will.

LEHMAN: Good. Now, listen to me, fellow oddball, how'd you like to work on Broadway?

ED: Right, moving sets.

LEHMAN: Never. That's a union job! You know my dear friend John Gielgud?

ED: To you, he's a friend, to me he's maybe the greatest actor in the world!

LEHMAN: Well, he also directs: Shakespeare, Sophocles, and now he's directing an American musical.

ED: Interesting...

LEHMAN: Starring: Debbie Reynolds!

ED: Sir John Gielgud is directing Debbie Reynolds?

LEHMAN: It's a revival of the biggest Broadway hit of 1919: a show called *Irene (sings)* "I'm always chasing rainbows."

ED: Great song.

LEHMAN: So is "Alice Blue Gown," but the rest is muck, and that's where you come in. They need someone up in Toronto to write additional lyrics—I recommended you.

ED: *(Disappointed)* Just lyrics. It wouldn't be my music—

LEHMAN: Picky, picky! How many Broadway offers have you turned down this week?

ED: *(Complete turnaround)* You're right—absolutely. It's a great opportunity. I'll get to work with Sir John Gielgud. *(Beat)* And Debbie Reynolds.

LEHMAN: And if it's a hit...

ED: I could quit my job. Just one thing...

(LIGHT CHANGE, isolating ED. *MUSICAL GLISS.* LEHMAN *freezes as* ED *turns to listen to:)*

FELICIA (VO):
           You can have a two-week leave, one time only. And when you come back, you're gonna turn every cast album in our catalogue into an all-string instrumental for lovers!

(MUSIC: Schmaltzy string instrumental of "I'm Always Chasing Rainbows")

ED: STOP!

(LIGHTS BACK)

When do I start?

LEHMAN: Sir John wants you up there immediately.

ED: I'm packing my *Wood's Rhyming Dictionary* and I'm on my way. By train. I'm going to be a big help to him.

LEHMAN: Ed—Sir John is a highly accomplished director.

ED: Of course, Lehman, but this is his first musical. I can walk him through the basic rudiments of good phrasing, talk him through the dynamics of orchestrations and—

LEHMAN: Ed—

ED: And explain how certain sequins on a dress can overwhelm a ballad, and I can really help him with—

LEHMAN: DON'T DO IT AGAIN!
BANISH THE THOUGHT
PUT IT RIGHT OUT OF YOUR MIND!

ED: I know comedy. And comedy has to be lit very caref—

LEHMAN: TEDDY BEAR, EDDIE BEAR
LEAVE THE FUNNY BEHIND . . .

ED: I was rereading this Jean Rosenthal book on lighting. You know how they have this theory about pink gels being good for women of a certain age, well, I'm thinking coral. *(Pulling the skin on his face up grotesquely)* It's like a face-lift for the eyes...

LEHMAN: DON'T DO IT THEN COUNT TO TEN ...

ED: I better get up there fast.

LEHMAN: THEN...

ED: This guy needs me!

   (ED *exits*)

LEHMAN: *(Calling out after him)* DON'T DO IT ...
           DON'T DO IT ...

           Oh, well. Maybe it'll work out. Right, and I'm the Queen of Rumania.

   (*BLACKOUT.*)

SCENE 8

TORONTO, 1972

OUTSIDE THE O'KEEFE CENTRE

(We hear the play-out music for Irene, *as* CHARLEY, LUCY, FELICIA, *and* MONA *enter, carrying* Playbills *and looking for* ED.*)*

LUCY: So did you see him?

MONA: Nope. I checked out every guy in the lobby.

FELICIA: I'll bet you did, honey.

BOBBY: *(Entering with* LEHMAN*)* I left him a note at the stage
           door—

CHARLEY: Hope we didn't miss him.

LEHMAN: He's probably backstage giving notes to Sir John.

*(ED enters, sees the group and tries to leave, hoping not to have
been spotted.)*

LEHMAN: There you are!

*(The group enthusiastically shows its support. Overlapping ad
libs, e.g., "Great work," "D'ya hear the laughs?" "Your name in the
program!" "Edward 'L.' Kleban: 'L?'")*

LUCY: The first one to actually write for a Broadway show!
           Told ya so.

ED: The whole gang . . . I knew I should've stopped you
           from coming all the way to Toronto!

ALL: Are you kidding? Try to have kept us away.

FELICIA: A 1919 musical in 1972? Now, that's progress!

BOBBY: We've been looking all over for you—no one knew
           where you were.

ED: Well, you know me, I like to keep a low profile.

BOBBY: Since when?

LEHMAN: I really must go backstage and congratulate Sir John. Coming, Ed?

ED: That thug guarding the stage door would have me on toast.

LEHMAN: What?

(*The group jumps in: overlapping ad libs, e.g., "Opening night nerves," "What thug?" "Relax, Ed." "Hey, let Ed talk . . . "*)

ED: (*The jig is up*) Sir John banned me from the theater.

ALL: Oh, my God. Why? What happened, Ed?

ED: I have no idea! I just made a few suggestions—

ALL: (*Completely understanding the problem immediately*) Oh.

LUCY: I'm so sorry, Ed. C'mon—someone around here must know where there's a bar in this godforsaken city—

BOBBY: How about the King Edward. Martinis all around?

ALL: Yeah, sure.

LEHMAN: You coming, Bobby?

ED: You go on ahead, and I'll be along in a little bit.

(*They all EXIT, except for* BOBBY *and* LUCY)

LUCY: Ed? (ED *is too stunned to respond*)

BOBBY: It's okay, Luce.

(Recognizing that BOBBY *is a comfort to* ED, LUCY *EXITS)*

ED: *(Trying to not feel sorry for himself, and failing)*
             I STAY LIGHT ON MY FEET . . .
             I STAY LIGHT ON MY FEET . . .

BOBBY: *(Cheering up Ed)* AND GIVE 'EM THAT
             DAH, DAH, DAH DAH,
             DAH, DAH, DAH, DAH,
             DAH, DAH, DAH!

BOBBY AND ED:
             FLAT-FOOT FLOOGIES FINISH UP LAST
             MOST OF THEM ARE LIVING ON SPAM

ED: THAT'S WHY LIGHT ON MY FEET IS WHAT I . . .

(ED can't quite finish the line when SOPHIE *enters, carrying a Playbill)*

SOPHIE: Congratulations, Eddie.

(UNDERSCORING: "One More Beautiful Song")

ED: Sophie!

BOBBY: I am so glad you are here. *(Out of Ed's earshot)* Perfect timing. I'll be at the King Eddie bar. Great to see you, Sophie.

(BOBBY exits)

ED: It's been a long time.

SOPHIE: Two years.

ED: —and seven months . . .

SOPHIE: I sat in the balcony. I was really proud of you.

ED: *(Angry)* Tell that to Lord High-and-Mighty.

SOPHIE: What?

ED: I'm banned from the theater.

SOPHIE: Why?

ED: It seems some people thought I was a pain in the ass.

SOPHIE: You? NO!!

ED: Can you believe it? I just made a few suggestions here
            and there—

SOPHIE: Told everyone how to do their jobs, did you?

ED: Not everyone. But the ushers really shouldn't let peo-
            ple walk in front of them when they're showing them
            to their—

SOPHIE: Eddie—

(They both laugh)

ED: I don't know, Sophie. I've been thinking. I love the
            theater, but maybe it's just not for me.

SOPHIE: Eddie, your work has integrity. And wit. And that's
            very rare. So stop shooting yourself in the foot.

ED: Maybe I should quit *Irene* and go back to New York
            and produce other people's albums.

SOPHIE: You got it backward. I think you should quit your job,
            stay here and work things out with this director.

ED: Quit my job?

SOPHIE: You're never going to be a professional unless you do
           this full time.

ED: What if the show's a flop? I'll be out on my can,
           broke, a failure ... I'll wind up in the cookie jar play-
           ing show tunes for the loonies.

SOPHIE: They always liked your songs.

ED: Forget it, Sophie. I'm going to go back to New York,
           close the door, and be with my piano.

SOPHIE: You're stronger than you think. Take a risk.

ED: How will I survive?

SOPHIE: You won't starve.

ED: What if I never get my music on?

SOPHIE: What if I never find a cure for cancer? I don't give up.
           It's my work. What I do. Songwriting is what you do.
           Remember that song you wrote for "Merton of the
           Movies?"

           FOLLOW, THE BEND IN THE RIVER
           GET WHERE YOU'RE GOING TO BE ...

ED: Soph, I don't need to be musically quoted right now.

SOPHIE: FOLLOW THE WIND IN THE VALLEY
           OVER THE HILL TO THE SEA

ED: Sophie, I am begging you to stop—

SOPHIE: ONLY THE HEAVENS TO GUIDE YOU

YONDER . . . WHEREVER YOU ROAM
Now here's the good part. Sing it with me.
BUT IF YOU FOLLOW YOUR STAR . . .

(ED doesn't react)

Eddie!

(She pushes him and he joins her)

ED & SOPHIE:
FOLLOW YOUR STAR
YOU'LL FIND HOME

ED: YOU'LL FIND . . .

(Quietly at first, and then with mounting enthusiasm)

Words and music. I love them. And especially what
happens when you put them together into songs.
And sing them, in a large building, in a central part of
town, in a dark room, as part of a play, with a lot of
people listening, who have all paid a great deal to get
in . . .

SOPHIE: *(Having fun with him)* Really? I had no idea!

(ED is totally "fixed"—excited by his new found hope.)

ED: ONLY THE HEAVENS TO GUIDE YOU
          YONDER . . . WHEREVER YOU ROAM

SOPHIE: BUT IF YOU FOLLOW YOUR STAR

ED: FOLLOW YOUR STAR

(He looks at SOPHIE, realizing what she's just done for him.

SOPHIE *beams.)*

TOGETHER:
>YOU'LL FIND HOME
>YOU'LL FIND . . .

*(*BOBBY *ENTERS carrying a note)*

BOBBY: Ed—the assistant stage manager was looking for you at the King Eddie—said Sir John told him to get this to you pronto.

ED: Sir John has probably gotten over our little contretemps and wants to meet back at the hotel. The new me: solving problems, not making them. *(He reads the note)* "Three things. One: You're a talented son of a bitch. Two: Pity you're impossible."

SOPHIE: Pity.

ED: "Three: You're . . . " *(His hand drops, still holding the note)*

SOPHIE: Eddie? *(She takes the note and reads the end)* Oh, Eddie. He fired you.

*(*ED *is stock still, in shock.* BOBBY *doesn't know what to say)*

BOBBY: *(With genuine caring)* Sophie?

SOPHIE: It's all right Bobby, I got it covered. We'll see you at the hotel.

*(*BOBBY *doesn't move)*

>Bobby, go.

(BOBBY *exits. Throughout the following,* SOPHIE *very calmly looks* ED *squarely in the face and reasons with him.* ED *remains in his own world, immobile.*)

> It's okay, Eddie. It's going to be okay. C'mon, I'll take you back to your hotel. You need a good night's sleep. We'll call your doctor and it'll all be fine. There'll be other shows. You're going to be fine, Eddie. I promise.
>
> YOU'LL FIND HOME . . .

(ED'S FRIENDS, *the* COMPANY, *enter in their memorial clothes. They stand at a distance from* ED, *echoing their words from the mental hospital*)

COMPANY: BESIDE THE FOUNTAIN IN THE GARDEN OF THE HOSPITAL . . .

(EDDIE, *still frozen, notices* DR. NODINE *very close to him and stares at him.*)

SOPHIE: (*Trying, gently, to engage Ed*) YOU'LL FIND HOME . . .

(SOPHIE *leads* ED *away from* DR. NODINE. *The underscore continues, with "Follow Your Star" morphing into the "One" vamp from* A Chorus Line *as* SOPHIE *helps* ED *offstage and the curtain slowly falls.*)

ACT II

SCENE 1

THE SHUBERT THEATRE, 1988; MANHATTAN, 1973
THE MEMORIAL

(LIGHTS UP as BOBBY *enters, holding a conductor's baton. He addresses us—the memorial audience.)*

BOBBY: Hi! I've already made my speech and everything. But the P.S. 114 Alumni Orchestra asked me to conduct a musical tribute to their famous alumnus, Ed Kleban. *(Introducing the orchestra)* The P.S. 114 orchestra—

*(*BOBBY *raises* HIS *baton and the orchestra begins playing a slow, amateurish, out-of-tempo ENTR'ACTE. The ghost of* ED *comes on and listens for a bit, becoming visibly upset. Finally,* ED *starts conducting the orchestra behind* BOBBY*, and damned if the music doesn't brighten and even swing by the end. Though a bit baffled—the band never played this well before—*BOBBY *finishes conducting with a flourish.* ED *falls back into the shadows as* MONA *takes the podium and applauds the orchestra.)*

MONA: Thank you, Bobby, and the P.S. 114 Orchestra. I know that Ed would've been touched. Particularly by the end of it.

BOBBY: Thanks, Mona.

*(*BOBBY *exits)*

MONA: *(To the memorial audience)* I'll tell ya one thing about Ed: once you were in his life, you were friends forever. Even when he wasn't talking to you. But after that messy stuff with Sophie, Ed avoided me in class.

Then this producer I met gave me a shot at writing songs for *Captain Kangaroo*. I froze. Writer's block. *(Shrugs innocently)* Nothing came out of my pouch. Two in the morning, it pops into my head to call Ed. He told me to come right over, so I did. And he gave me a very private songwriting lesson. Ed was so proud when Mr. Moose sang my Chipper Moose song! But after that "Debbie Reynolds" thing, he stopped returning my calls. We were all really worried about Ed. Then one day—I was playing piano for a tap class "up a steep and very narrow stairway."

(Underscoring: a stop-time version of "Light on My Feet" is played on the piano, as if in a tap dance class. Upstage, in single file, a couple of tap students [played by FELICIA *and* LUCY*] tap across the stage. The final tapper is—*ED*! As he taps offstage,*

MONA: *(calls after him)* Ed?

ED: *(Tapping backward toward* MONA*)* Mona!

MONA: You dropped off the planet—

ED: Tell you a secret: It felt like I did. Tried to get myself locked up in a mental hospital, but the doctor threw me out! Said half the people in New York were crazier than me!

MONA: And you do a groovier buck-and-wing!

ED: Working at it. Besides, directors and choreographers have this secret shuffle-step language—and the next time I get a chance to write songs for a Broadway show, I'm gonna know it—and I won't make an ass of myself! Again.

MONA: You're like a new person—you're so "up"!

ED: I quit my job! I'm broke, but I'm writing songs all the time! All the time! Except for tap class Tuesday, group therapy Thursday, the workshop Friday, and shrink every hour on the hour. Oh—I've also taken up napping, every afternoon, one to three. My doctor told me to take up jogging—I've lost five pounds!

MONA: You look great!

ED: I'VE BEEN FAT
I'VE BEEN THIN
THIN IS BETTER
I'VE BEEN OUT
I'VE BEEN IN
IN IS BETTER
I HAVE LOST
AND I HAVE WON
(LOSING ISN'T ANY FUN)

MONA: RAIN IS FINE, BUT WHEN IT'S DONE

BOTH: SUN IS BETTER

(MONA *exits;* FELICIA *enters.*)

FELICIA: Come back, Ed—I'll double your salary.

ED: It could never be enough!

FELICIA: I'VE BEEN POOR
I'VE BEEN RICH
RICH IS BETTER
FANCY OR NOT A STITCH
WHICH IS BETTER?

ED: Well, that depends . . .
I'VE BEEN HEALTHY AND IN PAIN
PAIN IS REASON TO COMPLAIN

ASK SOMEONE WHO'S BEEN INSANE
SANE IS BETTER!

FELICIA: *(Dancing seductively, she tantalizes* ED *with a contract
offering him a large salary at Columbia Records)*
YOU AND I IS BETTER
THINK AND YOU'LL AGREE
BETTER THAN JUST YOU
BETTER THAN JUST ME . . .

(As ED *reads the contract)*

ALL OUR DAYS
WHAT WE CALLED FUN WAS BETTER

ED: *(Rejecting Felica's contract)* ALL MY NIGHTS
EV'RY LAST ONE IS BETTER

FELICIA: GO IMPROVE ON BETTER
PUT IT TO THE TEST
WHEN YOU'VE CONVALESCED
HERE'S WHAT I SUGGEST:
BETTER LOOK ME UP
AND SETTLE FOR THE BEST . . .

*(*FELICIA *exits.* FIRST GIRL *enters: long blonde hair, sexy dress)*

FIRST GIRL: Loved your songs. I woke up humming "Paris
Through the Window." See you—

ED: Tuesday.

*(*FIRST GIRL *freezes, putting on an earring)*

I'VE BEEN GOOD
I'VE BEEN BAD
BAD IS BETTER

> NEED'S OKAY
> HAVING JUST HAD IS BETTER

(SECOND GIRL *enters, putting on lipstick.*)

SECOND GIRL:
> I woke humming "Paris." See you?

ED: Wednesday.

(SECOND GIRL *freezes opposite* FIRST GIRL. ED *continues singing, standing between the two* GIRLS.)

> I'VE BEEN FIRE, I'VE BEEN ICE
> I'VE BEEN NAUGHTY, I'VE BEEN NICE
> I'VE BEEN NAUGHTY ONCE OR TWICE
> TWICE IS BETTER!

FIRST GIRL & SECOND GIRL:
> YOU AND I IS BETTER
> IT'S A BETTER TUNE
> BETTER SOON THAN LATE
> BETTER NOW THAN SOON
> THAN SOON . . .

(FIRST GIRL *and* SECOND GIRL *exit.* LEHMAN & THE CLASS *burst onstage dressed for* ED'*s birthday party, circa 1973.*)

BOBBY: Surprise!

ALL: LIFE IS SHORT
           WHAT IS TODAY
           IS BETTER!

BOBBY: Hey, Happy Birthday!

ALL: DON'T BE LONG—
              RUN THE WHOLE WAY
              IS BETTER . . .

MONA: PUNISHMENT AIN'T AS GOOD AS CRIME

FELICIA: LATE IS BORING, TRY ON TIME

LEHMAN: FREE VERSE LACKS A CERTAIN CHIME

ALL: RHYME IS BETTER

FELICIA: I started my own label!

CHARLEY: I just scored the new Sydney Pollack film!

LUCY: I'm playing Ado Annie on the road!

LEHMAN: I'm writing a book about how to write musicals!

MONA: I wrote a song for Bunny Rabbit!

BOBBY: I play drums for Bunny Rabbit!

ED: Barbra Streisand is recording one of my songs!

   (All but CHARLEY *"OOOH" as . . .)*

CHARLEY: How'd you get that . . . ?

COMPANY: CHARLEY!

ALL: YOU AND I IS BETTER
              MORNING, NIGHT AND NOON
              BETTER SOON THAN LATE
              BETTER NOW THAN SOON . . .

(Abrupt LIGHT CHANGE. We are in the middle of the party. Piano-bar type underscoring is heard.)

ED: Hey, guys. What's shaking?

LEHMAN: *(Taking* ED *aside. The following lyrics are sung out of tempo, "ad lib" style)* Dear boy,
IF IT'S GOOD,
BREAKING THE NEWS IS BETTER
IF IT'S BAD,
SHAKING THE BLUES IS BETTER ...

Barbra cut your song from her album.

ED: Goddamn it, I counted on it!

BOBBY: Maybe Debbie Reynolds will be interested!

ED: CHECKERS DON'T COMPARE WITH CHESS
"MAYBE" LACKS THE PUNCH OF "YES"
I'll sue!

LEHMAN: Don't be a hothead.
WAR CAN BE AN AWFUL MESS
GUESS WHAT'S BETTER ...

ED: Thank God I only spent seventy-five thousand hours writing the damn thing.

LEHMAN: You're paying your dues.

ED: They better cover medical benefits for my shrink. Goddamn it, will anyone ever hear my songs?

LEHMAN: Take it easy, Ed.

BOBBY: There's more to life than a song—women, for example.

ED: I date every night.

BOBBY: So?

ED: Variations on a theme. But, well—

LEHMAN: Lordy! He's coming out!

ED: No, Lehman. I'm straight—I can't help it. I've been to
           all the best doctors.

BOBBY: Then what?

ED: There's one woman ...

BOBBY: Sophie?

ED: I just don't know how she feels about me.

BOBBY: Unless you try, you're never gonna know.
           Take it from me ...
           IN A RACE
           VERY LONG STRIDES ARE BETTER
           IF YOU'RE SMALL
           VERY SHORT BRIDES ARE BETTER ...

    (IN TEMPO)

COMPANY: PLEASE RETURN TO BETTER
           IT'S HER FOND REQUEST
           HERE'S WHAT I SUGGEST:
           BRING IT ALL ON HOME
           AND SETTLE FOR THE BEST!

    (COMPANY *dances toward* ED, *encouraging him to contact*
    SOPHIE*)*

           IT'S A CINCH
           PEOPLE IN PAIRS IS BETTER
           IN A PINCH
           SOMEONE WHO CARES IS BETTER!

ED: Okay, I'll call her!

COMPANY: DARLING, LOVE IS BETTER
               AND IT'S TIME YOU GUESSED
               WHEN YOU'VE CONVALESCED
               HERE'S WHAT I SUGGEST
               TAKE A BIG DEEP BREATH
               AND SETTLE FOR
               THE BESSSSSSSSSSSSSSSSST!

SCENE 2

SOPHIE'S LABORATORY, 1973

(SOPHIE, *wearing a lab coat, eyeglasses dangling from a chain around her neck, is looking through a microscope as* ED *enters. He is panting, out of breath.*)

SOPHIE: *(Continuing to look through her microscope)* Whoever that is, close the door behind you! Can't you read the sign?

ED: "Dr. Sophie Callan—Research Oncologist" and Muse of Song.

SOPHIE: Eddie! What a surprise!

ED: You moved your lab to the seventeenth floor.

SOPHIE: Right.

ED: You take an elevator to the seventeenth floor.

SOPHIE: So?

ED: You know how I feel about elevators—

SOPHIE: You didn't—

ED: I'm not sure I'll ever use my legs again.

SOPHIE: You walked up seventeen flights of—

ED: Thirteen. I stopped on the landing for a cigarette, then I crawled up the last four. You gotta light?

SOPHIE: No way. I spend my life looking through a microscope watching cells deviate, and here you are, my oldest and dearest—

ED: HELP! Please! Not the smoking speech again!

SOPHIE: How can I sit by and watch—

ED: You're looking at a man who walked up seventeen flights of stairs!

SOPHIE: Thirteen.

ED: I cut back from two packs to one pack. And I only smoke filters. And only when I'm writing.

SOPHIE: Or after dinner. Or on the telephone. Or in a meeting.

ED: (*Trying to change the subject*) What kind of microscope is that?

SOPHIE: I know you, Ed. The only time you don't smoke is in a theater. Or when you're sleeping. Or napping.

ED: Look at how cute you are, talking about cells and microscopes and deviated whatnots—

SOPHIE: I am totally serious here—

ED: *(Trying to win her back)*
            OBSERVE HER BOUNCING ALONG

SOPHIE: You're changing the subject.

ED: INDISPUTABLY THE NEATEST TRICK IN SIGHT
            WHY, EV'RY BREATHING MALE
            HAS SUDDENLY GRINNED
            TO SEE HER BLITHELY SAILING
            INTO THE WIND
            WITH SUCH UNSPEAKABLE GRACE . . .

SOPHIE: Oh, right—

ED: LITTLE BOYS GO OUT AND BUY THEMSELVES
                LONG PANTS!
            THEY ALL WANT TO KISS HER
            DON'T BLINK OR YOU'LL MISS HER
            SHE IS MY SCINTILLATING SOPHIE,
            QUEEN OF THE DARLING DEBUTANTES

SOPHIE: Debutantes? Talk about regression—Eddie, we are
            both in our thirties—well in our thirties—

ED: AND THOUGH HER DADDY IS IN SULPHUR
            AND HER MOMMY IS INSANE
            STILL, THERE'S NO DOUBT
            SHE'S COMING OUT . . .
            Dance with me, Soph!

      (ED *spins* SOPHIE *around the lab*)

ED: I'LL LAY YOU SEVEN TO ONE THAT SHE MUST
            HAVE SPENT HER JUNIOR YEAR IN FRANCE

(Still dancing with SOPHIE, ED *becomes increasingly short of breath)*

> THE WORLD'S HER COTILLION

SOPHIE: *(Playing with* ED *)* I'M ONE IN A MILLION!

ED: SHE IS MY SCINTILLATING SOPHIE
QUEEN OF THE DARLING
SCINTILLATING SOPHIE
QUEEN OF THE DARLING DEBUTANTES!

(He collapses in SOPHIE*'s arms, and, immediately, he begins to cough quite badly)*

SOPHIE: Cigarettes, Eddie. What am I going to do with you?

ED: Make mad passionate love to me, and then check my cells for deviation?

SOPHIE: Eddie!

ED: Okay. I'll quit smoking.

SOPHIE: Really?

ED: Yes. Sophie, my sweet Sophie, how about giving it another try?

SOPHIE: Us?

ED: "Us"—I like the sound of "us."

SOPHIE: Since we split up a hundred years ago, you've had how many—thirteen girlfriends?

ED: Fourteen. Mona has a twin. But no matter how many women I date, I'm lonely.

SOPHIE: Maybe you should try being alone. Maybe that's the only way you'll finish *Gallery*.

ED: I'm writing like crazy—ha! It's the only thing that keeps me sane—but I need someone to inspire me— I need love—I need you, my beauteous Sophie.

SOPHIE: *(Pulling back her hair from her ears)* Beauteous? Look—gray. And I just got bifocals.

ED: That's too bad, 'cause I'm at the peak of desirability. Paunchy, bald, blind—and I'm getting a major sty in my right eye—

SOPHIE: Let me see—*(she looks in his eye and takes out an eyelash)* It's just an eyelash. *(she holds it out on her finger)* Make a wish.

ED: I wish you'd reconsider. *(He blows on the eyelash)* I'm a different guy, Soph. No more Mr. Self-Involved, only worrying about my phobias and my career. Now I'm only a narcissist.

SOPHIE: My favorite narcissist.

ED: C'mon, Soph, whadaya say?

SOPHIE: Oh, Eddie, you know I'm really very fond of you.

ED: Fond? I'm "fond" of artichokes. We used to be crazy about each other. Oh, brother. It's the money, right? Now that I quit my job I'm just an unemployed, broke, no-talent loser who blew his big chance. Right?

SOPHIE: Wrong. You're—

ED: *(Cutting her off)* I'm a would-be wanna-be and you don't believe in me anymore, right?

SOPHIE: Wrong, wrong, wrong—this isn't about you. *(Straightforward)* I'm involved.

ED: Who is he? I'll strangle him with cassette tape.

SOPHIE: Oh, Eddie.

ED: C'mon, the truth: Deep down, underneath it all, we never stopped caring about each other.

SOPHIE: Truth: You thought I had nothing to do but wait for you.

ED: Sophie, forget the past.

SOPHIE: Oh, God.

ED: Let's start fresh. Now we have another chance—let's not bungle it.

SOPHIE: I think we just found something harder than quitting smoking...
            WE HAD THE SMILES
            WE HAD THE TUNES
            WE HAD A MULTITUDE OF LOVELY AFTER-
                NOONS
            AND COME TO THINK OF IT
            IT WAS THE NEXT BEST THING TO LOVE
            AND THOUGH WE FOUGHT
            THERE WAS NO PAIN
            THE SEX WAS GOOD BUT NEVER GREAT
            NEED I EXPLAIN?
            AND COME TO THINK OF IT
            IT WAS THE NEXT BEST THING TO LOVE
            SOMETHING ALWAYS MISSING
            CHRISTMAS IN L.A.
            WE COULD GET TO APRIL
            NOT TO MAY

AND SO AT LAST
WE LET IT GO
BECAUSE IT DOESN'T TAKE TWO
GENIUSES TO KNOW
THAT WHEN YOU THINK OF IT
AND IT IS WELL WORTH THINKING OF
IT WAS THE NEXT ...
BEST ...
THING ...
TO ... LOVE.
COULDN'T TURN THE CORNER,
NEVER MADE SUBLIME
STILL,
WE SHOULD BE SO LUCKY ALL THE TIME
SO NO REGRETS
FORGET THE TEARS
I KNOW A DOZEN GIRLS WHO'D RUN WITH
    THIS FOR YEARS
AND COME TO THINK OF IT
I GUESS THE NEXT BEST THING TO LOVE

IS ALSO LOVE.
IS ALSO LOVE.

(JEAN-CLAUDE *enters, everything that* ED *isn't: suave and confident. He gives* SOPHIE *a bouquet of flowers*)

JEAN-CLAUDE:
    Mon Papillon! Voila! Un petit cadeau!

(JEAN-CLAUDE *embraces* SOPHIE.)

SOPHIE: They're gorgeous! Jean-Claude—this is my forever
    friend, Eddie.

JEAN-CLAUDE:
    Sophie tells me you're quite the artiste! (*Shaking* ED*'s
    hand*) Jean-Claude Chevray.

ED: I know that name.

SOPHIE: *The New York Times*—Jean Claude just made a major
           discovery in astrobiology.

ED: Astrobiology?

JEAN-CLAUDE:
           I've heard so much about you.

   (LIGHTS BLACK OUT on SOPHIE *and* JEAN-CLAUDE, *leaving*
   ED *alone in a tight spot.)*

ED: FLAT-FOOT FLOOGIES FINISH UP LAST
           MOST OF THEM ARE LIVING ON SPAM—

JEAN-CLAUDE (OS):
           I've heard so much about you.

ED: THAT'S WHY LIGHT ON MY FEET IS WHAT I—

LIMBO MEMORIAL

   (LIGHT CHANGE. The COMPANY *enters. Their judgment of*
   ED *echoes in his ears.)*

FELICIA: Didn't get what he wanted.

LEHMAN: He was blocked.

MONA: It was the money.

FELICIA: Too selfish to have kids.

LEHMAN: Wasted his potential.

MONA: Not marriage material.

ED: *(Screams, trying to obliterate the voices in his head)* Damn it, Sophie! How could you!

(ED clutches his heart as the scene changes to . . .)

SCENE 3

CENTRAL PARK, 1973.

(MIDDAY, bright, sunny. ED *is stooped over, short of breath, as* LUCY, *carrying a textbook, accidentally meets up with him.)*

LUCY: Ed! Are you okay?

ED: Thank God! Luce! It suddenly occurred to me, what if I have a heart attack in the middle of Central Park?

LUCY: You have heart problems?

ED: No, no, nothing like that. Just these little pseudo-teensy weensy cardiac events. *(He clutches his heart tightly.* LUCY *"gets it.")*

LUCY: Sophie?

ED: Over. She found this astro-nuclear-bio-hoo-hah and they're in outer space.

LUCY: That roast chicken offer of yours still good?

ED: Aw, Luce. I'm trouble. Anyway, it's against Rule 33: Actresses are trouble.

LUCY: No problem. I'm giving up the theater. No more third redhead from the left. I'm studying to be a therapist.

ED: I can see that. Any discounts for broke songwriter
           friends?

LUCY: For you, sure.

ED: Thanks. *(New idea)* But wait—before you retire,
           would you help audition my music for this little Off-
           Broadway show? You sing so great.

LUCY: Sure. I'll consider it my swan song—

ED: Thanks. I'm counting on you. Oh. And that leather
           skirt you're wearing—don't.

BLACKOUT

SCENE 4

MICHAEL BENNETT'S STUDIO, 1973

*(A rehearsal studio with full-length mirrors, a piano, a bench.
The lighting is dim, atmospheric. A small tape recorder on the
piano is playing a worktape of ED singing and playing "Paris
Through the Window."*

MICHAEL BENNETT, *32, wiry, intense, a charismatic dancer-
choreographer-director, is dancing to the song, watching himself
in the mirror. Throughout the scene, he holds a cigarette in his
hand. Self-absorbed,* MICHAEL *continues dancing, as* ED
and LUCY *enter.)*

ED (VO: ON TAPE):
           PARIS ON THE EIGHTEENTH AUGUST
           PARIS WITH THE GARBAGE, FINE
           PARIS THROUGH THE WINDOW
           AND THEY MISSED IT
           THAT PARIS WAS MINE!

(As ED *enters, he listens to the tape)*

ED: *(Referring to his voice on the tape)* I hate when I'm flat.

MICHAEL: A perfectionist—like me. Someone get the lights while I turn this damn thing off. (MICHAEL *turns off the tape)*

*(*LUCY *turns on the lights as* MICHAEL *recognizes* LUCY *)*

MICHAEL: LUCY? Lucy Chaprakowski?

LUCY: Not since you were Mickey DiFiglia!!

MICHAEL: *(Remembering the old show they were in together)* Bajour! *(Dancing)* EVERYBODY'S LOOKING FOR THE BIG BAJOUR!

LUCY: *(Dancing with* MICHAEL *)* EVERYBODY'S LOOK-ING FOR THE ONE BIG BREAK—!

*(*LUCY *and* MICHAEL *hug)*

MICHAEL: All those years in the chorus together! How long ago was that?

LUCY: Don't ask. You've done pretty well for yourself since then. Choreographing, directing. Two Tonys?

ED: Actually, three.

MICHAEL: But who's counting? (MICHAEL *introduces himself and shakes hands with* ED *)* Michael Bennett. Classy name, huh?

ED: Ed Kleban. Actually Lord Kleban, but I don't use the title.

MICHAEL: By the way, she's a terrific singer.

ED: I know.

LUCY: What Michael's not saying is that I can't dance.

MICHAEL: Oh, come on—"As if dancing were everything." Who said that? *(To* LUCY, *referring to* ED *)* He's good, huh?

LUCY: The best!

MICHAEL: *(Pointedly, to* ED *)* Good. Good. I only work with the best.

(MICHAEL *ushers them deeper into the room, cigarette pack in hand, taking command of the meeting.)*

So, let's talk about my Dancer Project. It's about a group of chorus kids—and I can tell you from years as a hoofer, they get treated like cattle.

LUCY: I can vouch for that.

MICHAEL: So last month, about twenty of us got together for an encounter session. Everyone talked about their childhood, blah, blah, blah—about dancing, blah, blah, blah. I got it all on tape. I don't even know if it's a musical, but Joe Papp at The Public Theater is giving me a workshop. And I'm looking for a songwriter to help explore the possibilities.

ED: I'll check my schedule. *(Without a beat)* I'm available.

MICHAEL: Good. So. You're gonna play some more songs for me?

(MICHAEL *taps his fingers restlessly.)*

ED: We'll start with "Children's Games," from a musical
            I'm trying to get on called *Gallery*.

(ED goes to the piano.)

            It's about this guy, Harold, who is having a nervous
            breakdown and hides out in an art gallery. He sees a
            Brueghel painting of grotesque children and thinks
            about killing himself.

MICHAEL: Gawd, I've just taken two bennies. Got anything with
            a little pep?

LUCY: Ed—let's do "Broadway Boogie Woogie." It's perfect!

ED: But we rehearsed the Brueghel. "Boogie Woogie's"
            the Mondrian, and the song is about—

(He finally "gets" the rightness of LUCY'S choice)

            Right. Hit it, Lucy.

*(A beat. MICHAEL watches as ED waits expectantly for LUCY to
sing. LUCY waits for ED to play the intro to the song. Finally . . .)*

LUCY: *(To ED)* Hit it!

ED: Oh, me. Right.

*(ED plays the piano as LUCY performs the number for
MICHAEL)*

LUCY: GOT UP AT EIGHT . . .
            DID MY HAIR . . .
            DID MY FACE SANG MY SCALES . . .
            LIMBERED UP AT THE BAR
            I GRABBED A CAB . . .

> TOOK MY PLACE IN THE LINE
> THEN THE MAN SAID THEY WANTED A STAR
> I GOT THE BROADWAY BOOGIE WOOGIE
> KNOWN AS "DON'T CALL US . . .
> WE'LL CALL YOU"
>
> I'M MUCH TOO TALL,
> MUCH TOO SHORT,
> MUCH TOO THIN,
> MUCH TOO FAT,
> MUCH TOO YOUNG FOR THE ROLE
> I SING TOO LOW,
> SING TOO HIGH, SING TOO LOUD
> "COULD YOU READ IT WITH A LITTLE
>   CONTROL?"
> I GOT THE BROADWAY BOOGIE WOOGIE
>   KNOWN AS . . .

MICHAEL & LUCY:
>   "DON'T CALL US . . . WE'LL CALL YOU"

MICHAEL: *(Pulling Lucy in to dance with him.)* C'mon, Lucy, lemme see you dance!

LUCY: Michael, you know I can't dance.

MICHAEL: I made Hepburn look good in *Coco!*

LUCY:
>   I KNOW I CAN DO REAL WELL
>   ALL I NEED'S A START
>   IF I'D ONLY JUST THIS ONCE
>   GET THE PART!
>
>   STILL, I TAKE LESSONS, GO TO CLASS,
>   STUDY VOICE
>   GO TO SLEEP WITH THE CREAM ON MY FACE
>   I GET TURNED DOWN AS A MATTER OF
>   COURSE

WHAT WOULD BERNHARDT HAVE DONE IN
    MY PLACE?
I GOT THE BROADWAY BOOGIE WOOGIE
AND I THINK I KNOW THE WAY THE WIND
    BLOWS
(FIX MY NOSE? . . . SHIT!)
I GOT THE BROADWAY BOOGIE WOOGIE
AND IF NOTHING TURNS UP I THINK THIS
    SHOW IS GONNA CLOSE
STILL, THEY ALWAYS TELL YOU IT'S HARD

(Spoken over music)

Maybe I'll just leave him my card . . .

(MUSICIAL BUTTON)

MICHAEL: Chaprakowski, thank you, darling.

LUCY: *(Joking)* Am I cut?

MICHAEL: Mind if I have a few words with Ed alone?

LUCY: Oh, sure.

ED: *(Whispering to* LUCY *)* Thanks Luce. Call ya later.

*(*LUCY *exits.)*

MICHAEL: It's like pornography.

ED: That bad.

MICHAEL: It's genius. I know it when I see it. You'll write fabulous lyrics for my new show.

ED: Yes, lyrics. And music, too.

MICHAEL: You know Marvin Hamlisch?

ED: Not personally.

MICHAEL: He's Viennese, and the music pours out of him like
            wasserschnitzel.

ED: What's wasserschnitzel?

MICHAEL: I don't know but they schnitzel everything over there.
            Your lyrics—his music. It'll be a sensational collabo-
            ration. *(He begins talking very fast, trying to railroad*
            ED *)* I'll set up a meeting next week—

ED: Michael—

MICHAEL: —you'll listen to the tapes—

ED: Michael—

MICHAEL: —we'll do a workshop next month at the Public.

ED: *(Losing it)* Michael! *(measured, but firm)* I appreciate
            the offer, but I'm a composer and my music means
            everything to me—no. No.

   (ED *heads for the exit)*

MICHAEL: *(stopping* ED *)* Ed, I promise, if you do lyrics for this
            show, the next musical I direct will be *Gallery.*
            Whadayasay?

   (ED *takes* MICHAEL'*s hand and shakes on the deal)*

ED: I look forward to working with Marvin.

MICHAEL: Good.

   (BLACKOUT)

SCENE 5

A CHORUS LINE *LIMBO*

THE PUBLIC THEATER, 1974-1975

(MICHAEL BENNETT, MARVIN HAMLISCH and ED, each in a separate LIMBO area. MARVIN, a composer, is 29 and tall and gangly, with the high-spirited enthusiasm of a Great Dane puppy.)

MARVIN: *(In separate limbos: to MICHAEL)* I gotta tell ya something...

MARVIN AND ED:
          I CAN'T STAND HIM!

(Underscoring: "Who Am I Anyway" from A Chorus Line. MAR-VIN *and* ED *each talk "privately" to* MICHAEL.*)*

MARVIN: Is he for real? The guy naps! Every day!

ED: He's crazier than me!

MARVIN: Three Oscars and he says my music won't work!

ED: Ten years learning to write theater songs! I'm not gonna write pop!

MARVIN: Who needs a hundred bucks a week? Chicken feed!

ED: I don't care how much I need the hundred bucks a week!

(MUSIC OUT; LIGHTS OUT on MICHAEL and ED.)

MEMORIAL LIMBO

MARVIN: Ya gotta understand, I was younger—like 29, and I was like ... like I am now but, ya know, more. I'd just come back from Hollywood, probably given up my next three pictures to write a musical with this guy, Ed Kleban. I mean, I'd heard Streisand sing one of his songs—what did he need me for? So I was very careful not to act like I was, ya know, this big deal Oscarwinner.

(MUSICAL Underscoring: "I Can Do That" from A Chorus Line*)*

MICHAEL'S STUDIO LIMBO

(ED enters, trying to get MICHAEL's attention, but MICHAEL never stops dancing in front of the mirrors)

ED: He's giving me palpitations.

MICHAEL: I know Marvin's like—off the leash, but he writes the best dance music in the biz. And ... *(Drawing it out)* ... THIS IS A DANCE MUSICAL, so Marvin is IN-DIS-PENSIBLE.

ED: But Michael, he—

MICHAEL: Go home, sleep on it, get laid, and if you still won't "play nice" with Marvin, DON'T COME BACK!

(ED exits. MARVIN enters, trying to get MICHAEL's attention as MICHAEL continues dancing.)

MARVIN: He's giving me ulcers.

MICHAEL: Ed Kleban? "The nap?" Puh-leese! But HE IS THE BEST LYRICIST SINCE STEVE SONDHEIM. By the way—*(MICHAEL comes to a full stop in mid-dance step. He eyeballs MARVIN)* he's not a bad composer either—

(He exits. LIGHT CHANGE.)

MARVIN: *(To the memorial audience)* Somehow—we started to write. On neutral ground. At my mother's house.

THE HAMLISCH APARTMENT

(The piano has pride of place. ED paces, grabs a crystal dish and uses it as an ashtray. MARVIN enters and grabs the crystal dish away from ED)

MARVIN: Hey—that's my mother's Czechoslovakian crystal dish!

ED: *(Grabbing the crystal dish away from MARVIN)* And I need it!

MARVIN: Give it to me!

ED: No.

MARVIN: Give it!

ED: No.

MARVIN: Give it!

ED: NO!

MARVIN: I'm telling.

(ED quickly gives the dish back)

ED: So, who goes first? Music or lyrics? Do you want me to write the music—sorry, LYRIC first—or, do you want to go first with the music?

MARVIN: This is how I like to do it. First, you give me a title. The music for the title is everything, I'm telling ya— then the rest just flows.

(MARVIN *sits at the piano*)

ED: *(Mimicking)* "Flows." Okay. You want a title? (ED *paces*) I did my own interviews with each of the dancers—I don't wanna mention names—and what these kids have in common is they had lousy, miserable, terrible, awful childhoods. The only time they were happy was at the ballet. So there's your title: "At the Ballet." *(Grabbing the crystal dish)* And I need that Czechoslovakian crystal dish.

MARVIN: I'll write quick, so you don't smoke up the house.

(He begins to improvise at the piano.)

First I gotta get the feel ... Da-da ... At the Ballet ...

(Continuing to find a musical feel)

Da-da-da . . . At the Ballet . . .

ED: *(Marvin continues to play as)* What I got here is foster homes ... orphanages ... incest ...

MARVIN: Wait a minute, wait a minute, I got it. Wait 'til you hear it. It's a killer!

(MARVIN *plays a catchy, very up, two-four tune*)

DA-DA-DA AT THE BALLET!
DA-DA-DA AT THE BALLET!

It's up there with Tschaikovsky—Rachmaninoff—

Beethoven—
DA-DA-DA AT THE BALLET,
AT THE BALLET!

(MARVIN *pauses, delighted with his tune, and looks to* ED, *anticipating that* ED *will be thrilled*)

ED: (*A beat, then*) No. That won't work.

MARVIN: That won't WORK?

ED: Think philandering fathers ...

(MARVIN, *baffled by* ED, *but willing to try again, improvises a revision ... *)

Frustrated mothers ...

(MARVIN *develops the revision*)

Alcoholic frustrated mothers.

(MARVIN *embellishes the revision*)

MARVIN: Got it! I'm done! (MARVIN *plays a serious dramatic tune*)

DA-DA-DA-DA-DA, AT THE BALLET!
DA-DA-DA-DA-DA, AT THE BALLET!

It's perfect! It's philandering fathers, frustrated mothers, orphanages and incest all rolled into one!

(MARVIN *continues to play, developing his masterpiece, as* ED *interjects the four words that are the kiss of death*)

ED: No. That won't work.

MARVIN: *(Bangs the piano)* What! That tune has so much pain in it, people are gonna want to check into a hospital after they hear it!

ED: Try Dancer 20.

MARVIN: *(Pissed, improvising angrily on the piano, silent-movie style)* What'd you find? White slavery? Raised by wolves? Bound and gagged and forced to listen to Jim Nabors polka records!

(MARVIN *plays a cheesy polka*)

ED: Watch it! (ED *sits on a stool, his back to* MARVIN) There's something one of the dancers said to me . . . *(He takes a Rodin "Thinker" pose, his head cupped in his hands, concentrating.* MARVIN *looks on, totally silent. After a few beats,* ED *turns to* MARVIN *and "shh's" him.)* Shh!

(MARVIN *is so exasperated, words fail him. He begins to play a few simple notes– the opening eight bars of "At the Ballet" that we know. He stops abruptly.)*

MARVIN: That's a "NO"—Right? *(Spells)* "N-O."

ED: *(After a beat)* I like it.

MARVIN: *(Sarcastic, to the heavens)* He likes it!

(*MUSICAL Underscoring: Trumpets blare "At the Ballet."* ED *moves to* SOPHIE'*s lab.)*

SOPHIE'S LAB LIMBO

(SOPHIE *enters.* ED *takes her hand as he attempts to do ballet-barre exercises.)*

ED: C'mon, Soph, ya gotta help me with my research.

SOPHIE: I haven't done this since Madame Bilchick's Academy
           on Fordham Road.

ED: *(Attempting first position)* Like this?

SOPHIE: *(Doing a respectable first position)* No, this is first
           position.

ED: Lucy's not supportive.

SOPHIE: (SOPHIE *goes to second position)* Now, second posi-
           tion.

ED: (ED *does an awkward second position as...*) Ow. Ow.
           Marvin's a maniac.

SOPHIE: Plié.

ED: (ED *does a plié)* Ow! Michael's a dictator.

SOPHIE: Relevé. (ED *does a relevé with* SOPHIE)

ED: There's no story. Michael wants it to feel like one big
           musical number, but it feels like one long turgid
           snooze.

SOPHIE: Merde.

ED: Huh?

SOPHIE: Bullshit. You're looking for a fall guy in case YOU fail.
           DON'T FUCK THIS UP!

ED: I NEVER LIKED YOU!

SOPHIE: Hop to it!

(SOPHIE exits)

A CHORUS LINE *LIMBO*

ED: *(Reading from a legal pad)*
"Everyone was beautiful at the ballet—
Scratch a duck, you always get a swan."
(He stops—questioning what he's just written)
"Scratch a duck?"
(Self-critical) Terrible.
(Writing) "A duckling always gets to be a swan."
(Assessing his work) Better.

(MARVIN enters.)

MARVIN: I came in on the red-eye from L.A. and I'm telling ya, I'm ready for a nap.

ED: It's been ten days and you don't return my phone calls!

MARVIN: C'mon, Ed, I was involved—don't you have a love life?

ED: Yes! But during my nap!

MARVIN: *(He is not going there)* Okay, show me the lyric.

ED: First eight:
"Everything was beautiful at the ballet
Graceful men lift lovely girls in white"

MARVIN: It fits perfectly with my music!

ED: Okay,—last eight:
"Everyone is beautiful at the ballet
Ev'ry prince has got to have his swan"

MARVIN: You're a goddamn poet!

ED: Well, the tune ain't bad either.

(MUSIC Underscoring: "At the Ballet")

MEMORIAL LIMBO

MARVIN: Now we were cooking—but here comes the incredi-
ble part: Ed had each piece of music I wrote assessed
by the BMI Workshop. It had a quality of, ya know,
the Emperor who went—*(He gives a thumbs down)*

DANCER LIMBO

(Three DANCERS *are revealed one by one, in silhouette.)*

DANCER ONE:
    I WAS PRETTY...

DANCER TWO:
    I WAS HAPPY...

DANCER THREE:
    I WOULD LOVE TO...

ALL THREE TOGETHER:
    AT... THE... BALLET...

A CHORUS LINE LIMBO

*(*ED *comes running on)*

ED: Marvin—

(A pregnant pause. Keeping MARVIN *in suspense.)*

MARVIN: Ya?

ED: They liked it!

MARVIN: Aha!

(*BLACKOUT on* MARVIN *and* ED)

THE MEMORIAL

(LUCY *stands in the golden memorial spotlight*)

LUCY: It was an exciting time—except when Ed blamed me
           for making him have a bad rhyme day. Ed was incred-
           ibly nervous, jumpy. He'd take these long walks at
           lunch and nobody could find him.

CHURCH LIMBO

(*MUSIC Underscoring:* "Nothing" *from* A Chorus Line)

ED: (*On his knees, praying. He makes a vague attempt at
           crossing himself*) Santa Maria, give me guidance. I'm
           not sure how to do this—I'm not Catholic, but this is
           the nearest house of worship to rehearsal, and I need
           all the help I can get. Not for me, but if anything
           comes of this little show, I swear on the heads of
           Abraham, Isaac, and my grandfather Nutty
           Klebansky, I'll find a way to give back. Sholom
           Aleichem, you're a saint to listen to me. And look, I
           know I can be controlling and a pain in the ass, but I
           promise, from now on I'll do anything, anything they
           ask of me.

(*MUSIC OUT. Lights up on* MARVIN.)

ED: I won't do it!

MARVIN: What's so terrible about writing a song that people can understand without knowing the plot? I don't get it.

ED: You've done a great job writing music that supports the story, Marvin. Why wreck it just to get a standard into the score?

MARVIN: A standard! We should be so lucky! One song, Ed—

ED: I like your tune, it's a good tune, but it ...

MARVIN WITH ED:
     ... WON'T WORK!

ED: And I refuse to do it!

  SOPHIE LIMBO

SOPHIE: *(Appears, admonishing* ED *)* EDDIE!!

ED: Song for Marvin:

  (BLACKOUT on MARVIN *and* SOPHIE *)*

     Kiss today goodbye ...
     (He begins to sing)
     THE SWEETNESS AND THE SORROW.
     WISH ME LUCK,
     THE SAME TO YOU,
     BUT I CAN'T REGRET
     WHAT I DID FOR .....

  *(*ED *can't get out the word "love."* MARVIN *enters and waits for* ED *to finish. Finally,* MARVIN *pointedly completes the line)*

MARVIN: —LOVE! WHAT I DID FOR ...

ED: *(a tad nauseated)*—LOVE...

(When they finally sing together, it is clear that they have over-come their difference and become first-rate collaborators, and true friends.)

TOGETHER: *(Acknowledging each other)* WHAT I DID FOR...
            LOVE...

(The vamp from A Chorus Line's *"One" leads us back to)*

A CHORUS LINE *LIMBO*

(The COMPANY *enters, as the dancers of* A Chorus Line, *with* MICHAEL *running a rehearsal)*

MICHAEL: Okay, everybody—Let's take it from the finale. Nice
          and easy. A five, six, seven, eight—

COMPANY: *(Sung without the familiar "sting" after the word
          "One")* ONE FABULOUS SENSATION,
          EVERY LITTLE STEP SHE TAKES...

MICHAEL: Hold it! Hold it! Hold it!

(As MUSIC continues under)

MARVIN: Give me a bang after "One."

MARVIN: A "bang"?

MICHAEL: Yeah. "ONE"—"BANG!"—"FABULOUS SENSA..."

MARVIN: Why?

MICHAEL: That's the way I want it.

MARVIN: Gotcha.

(MARVIN runs downstage to speak to musicians as MICHAEL *takes* ED *aside)*

MICHAEL: Ed—"Fabulous" and "sensation" are redundant.

ED: Right. They mean the same thing.

MICHAEL: I need a lyric rewrite NOW.

ED: After my nap.

MICHAEL: Forget the nap!

ED: Fine. No nap. Rewrite: "ONE SINGULAR SENSA-TION"...

MICHAEL: I like it—I like it a lot—

ED: *(To* MARVIN*)* Got him! "One" and "singular" are redundant!

MICHAEL: *(To the* COMPANY*)* Now, with the bang!

(The CHORUS DANCERS *grab motley rehearsal hats to use as props)*

MICHAEL: A five, six —A five, six, seven, eight—

CHORUS: ONE *(sting)* SINGULAR SENSATION!
             EVERY LITTLE STEP SHE TAKES—

MICHAEL: That is great. Listen up, everybody: The title isn't gonna be *Chorus Line.* It is *A Chorus Lin*e which will put us first in the ABC listings of Broadway shows, and we just may get there if you kids dance your feet off and don't fuck it up!

             Places! First preview! A five, six, seven, eight—

(MICHAEL, MARVIN, and COMPANY perform "One" as ED beams.)

CHORUS: ONE MOMENT IN HER PRESENCE
           AND YOU CAN FORGET THE REST.
           FOR THE GIRL IS SECOND BEST
           TO NONE, SON,
           OOH! SIGH! GIVE HER YOUR ATTENTION.
           DO . . . I . . . REALLY HAVE TO MENTION?
           SHE'S THE . . .
           SHE'S THE . . .
           HE'S THE . . . ONE!

SOPHIE: *(Stepping out the CHORUS, in character as SOPHIE)*
           Eddie, I'm so proud!

CHORUS: . . . ONE!

LUCY: *(Stepping out of the CHORUS, in character as LUCY)*
           That's my guy!

CHORUS: . . . ONE!

MICHAEL: I discovered him!

ALL: . . . ONE!

LEHMAN: *(Stepping out of the CHORUS, in character as LEHMAN)* My best student!

ALL: . . . ONE!

MONA: *(Stepping out of the CHORUS, in character as MONA)*
           I slept with him.

ALL: . . . ONE!

MARVIN: We did it, Ed!

ALL: ...ONE!

FELICIA: (*Stepping out of the* CHORUS, *in character as* FELI-
                 CIA) So, I was wrong.

ALL: ...ONE!

ED: My God.

ALL: (*To* ED) Okay, so are ya happy????

SCENE 6

TONY AWARDS LIMBO, 1975-1985

TONY EMCEE (VO):
                 And the Tony for best score goes to Marvin Hamlisch
                 and Edward Kleban—*A Chorus Line!*

(*All except* ED *exit.*)

ED: (*He mimes holding a Tony*) Thanks Marvin, thanks
                 Michael, and thanks to Joe Papp for giving me the
                 chance to work in the theater I love so much. Thanks
                 Lehman Engel, and ten years in the BMI Workshop
                 learning how NOT to write theater songs—thanks
                 Sophie, thanks Lucy...

                 I HAVE LOST
                 AND I HAVE WON—
                 —LOSING ISN'T ANY FUN—
                 RAIN IS FINE, BUT WHEN IT'S DONE—
                 SUN IS BETTER—

(LEHMAN *enters*)

LEHMAN: Thanks to Ed, my book on writing musicals is a best-seller!

(FELICIA *enters*)

FELICIA: Because of Ed, I love musicals! I'm producing a musical!

(Remainder of COMPANY *enter and congratulate* ED *on his success)*

ED & COMPANY:
    GO IMPROVE ON BETTER,
    PUT IT TO THE TEST!
    WHEN YOU NEED A REST,
    BETTER LOOK ME UP
    AND SETTLE FOR THE BEST—

ED: Lucy—*(*ED *takes* LUCY*'s hands in his.* LUCY *looks at* ED *adoringly)* OUT OF ALL THE PEOPLE IN THIS WORLD I CHOOSE YOU ...

Would you promise to live with me five—sorry, four days a week?

OUT OF ALL THE PEOPLE IN THIS WORLD
WHICH AMOUNTS TO QUITE A FEW ...

Do you promise to listen when I play the same song for hours? And not fall asleep?

WHETHER WE'RE WRONG OR RIGHT
WHETHER IT'S BLISS OR BLIGHT ...

Do you promise not to spend all the money I made from *A Chorus Line*, because I'm terrified I'll end up in the poorhouse?

LUCY: I do.

ED: OUT OF ALL THE PEOPLE IN THIS WORLD YOU

LUCY: *(To* ED*)* OUT OF ALL THE BLOSSOMS ON THE VINE YOU PICK ME
OUT OF ALL THE HEROES, FIRM AND FINE
AND THE ONES YOU CAN'T FORESEE

Edward, do you promise not to break up with me more than twice a week?

WHETHER IT'S GOOD OR BAD
WHETHER WE'RE MAD OR HAD

Do you promise not to fool around on the side, even on the two days a week we break up?

ED: *(A beat, then)* Maybe I should talk to my lawyer.

LUCY: *(Turning to EXIT)* Goodbye, Ed—

ED: Wait!—I do.

ED & LUCY: Scary! OUT OF ALL THE PEOPLE IN THE WORLD YOU

*(*ED *and* LUCY *embrace)*

LIMBO: THE NIGHTMARE, 1976-1985

(During this section, the music gets increasingly dissonant as, one by one, each of ED*'s new projects fizzles, and he struggles to keep singing. As each project dies, the title appears, as if on a marquee, projected on the back wall:* Gallery, The Heartbreak Kid, Musical Comedy, Scandal.*)*

MICHAEL-IN-LIMBO:
>   Ed, darling. *Gallery*'s just not my thing. I'm doing a
>   show about ballroom dancers.

ED:
>   You what? Oh, forget it! Joe Papp will give me a work-
>   shop at The Public Theater.
>   I STAY LIGHT ON MY FEET
>   I STAY LIGHT ON MY FEET
>   AND GIVE 'EM THAT
>   DAH-DAH-DAH-DAH
>   DAH-DAH-DAH-DAH
>   DAH-DAH-DAH-DAH

LEHMAN:
>   So *Gallery* bombed. Take a nap. Then start a new
>   show.

ED:
>   I will, Lehman. Neil Simon asked me to musicalize
>   one of his comedies on spec.
>   I STAY LIGHT ON MY FEET
>   I STAY LIGHT ON MY FEET
>   AND HIT 'EM WITH
>   SHU-DAH-BU-DWAH
>   SHU-DAH-BU-DWAH
>   SHU-DAH-BU-DWAH

MONA:
>   Your work on the Simon project was terrific, Ed!

ED:
>   (*To* MONA, *angrily*) I sent five songs to Doc Simon
>   —he never even responded!
>
>   WHEN DAME FORTUNE TOSSES ME A CURVE
>   I NEVER GIVE AWAY TO DESPAIR . . .

FELICIA:
>   A musical about the BMI Workshop?

LEHMAN:
>   Interesting songs, Ed. But the show just doesn't work.

ED:
>   I STAY LIGHT ON MY FEET—

I STAY LIGHT ON MY FEET—

MICHAEL: Ed, dahling, *Ballroom* was a bust. Want to write a new show together? Your music this time.

ED: *Gallery?*

MICHAEL: Maybe next year. This one's about free love. Orgies.

ED: Orgies just aren't my thing.

> BUT I LAND RIGHT ON MY FEET
> I LAND RIGHT ON MY FEET
> AND GO WITH THAT
> *(Overlapping* MARVIN*)*
> DAH-DAH-DAH-DAH
> DAH-DAH-DAH-DAH
> DAH-DAH-DAH . . .

MEMORIAL LIMBO

MARVIN: *(Overlapping as* ED *sings, he appears in golden memorial light)* I always thought we'd do another show together, ya know, composer and lyricist are like husband and wife. But we did get an Oscar nomination for a song in the movie of *A Chorus Line.* Ed got on a plane to fly out for the awards, but he freaked and made them let him off on the runway. Maybe he wasn't so crazy: We didn't win.

LUCY: *(In golden memorial light)* Ed got more and more phobic, wrote music obsessively. I thought he needed a vacation—just one weekend—two days. He said I was trying to keep him from his work—that I wasn't supportive. The only one he could trust was Sophie.

(Full stop. MUSIC OUT.)

SOPHIE LIMBO

(SOPHIE *enters.* COMPANY *remains onstage and observes)*

ED: Sophie, I work and work, nothing gets on! I'm losing
             it! I'm gonna wind up back in the nuthouse making
             ashtrays!

SOPHIE: You want the truth?

ED: Truth.

SOPHIE: You're afraid you're not going to top *A Chorus Line.*

ED: No.

SOPHIE: Didn't Marvin ask you to write with him? Didn't you
             meet with Richard Rodgers? Andrew Lloyd Webber?

ED: Andrew Lloyd Webber invited me to his hotel suite—
             first meeting, he's in his bathrobe, and barefoot!
             Anyway, I refuse to merely write lyrics!!!

SOPHIE: Well, maybe your music isn't as good as your lyrics.

(Everyone onstage looks at ED *)*

ED: *(Icy cold)* Don't. Ever. Talk. To. Me. Again.

SOPHIE: That's not what I meant to say...

ED: Our friendship is over.

COMPANY: GO IMPROVE... GO IMPROVE...

(ED exits)

SOPHIE: I'm not gonna be on that list of people you don't talk
            to—(Calling after him) You can't do this to me! Don't
            walk out, EDDIE! What are you doing? Don't do the
            iron door on me!

(SOPHIE exits. The COMPANY all speak to each other,
conversations overlapping)

FELICIA: What did Sophie know about music? She's a scientist.

MONA: I loved Ed's music.

BOBBY: We all did.

LUCY: No one but Ed could have written those songs.

FELICIA: So what happened? Why didn't the shows get on?

(COMPANY argues with each other)

LEHMAN: Stop. Please. The problem was never the music. He
            was terrified. Ed sabotaged every opportunity that
            came his way. It wasn't the writing. It was him. Let's
            move on, shall we?

(COMPANY exits as we hear:)

ED (OFFSTAGE):
            (Knocking furiously) Let me in! Let me in!

SCENE 7

SOPHIE'S LABORATORY, 1985

(SOPHIE, alone in her lab, on the telephone.)

SOPHIE: No, don't call the police. He's not a maniac—Let him
          in. (SOPHIE *hangs up the telephone. Thinks, then dials
          again*) Alex—hold my calls.

(She puts down the telephone. ED *enters, carrying a manila
envelope)*

ED: Those goons tried to stop me from running the serv-
          ice elevator.

SOPHIE: They're guards, Eddie. Anyway, I'm glad you're here.
          Let's talk rationally.

ED: *(Interrupting)* No. No. No. No ...

SOPHIE: What I was trying to say to you was ...

ED: *(Loud, final)* NO! I don't want to hear it. I'm not
          speaking to you.

SOPHIE: Fine. I'm very busy. I'm working with a live culture.

ED: So this is where live culture went when theater died.

SOPHIE: What's going on with you, Eddie?

ED: The other day, I thought I bit my tongue. So you
          know me, I make a big megillah out of it. I go to Dr.
          Stein. So Stein sends me to this big deal specialist, Dr.
          Conley.

SOPHIE: John Conley? The Chief of Head and Neck at St.
          Vincent's?

ED: *(He hands* SOPHIE *the manila envelope)* Right. Take a
          look at these slides. I needed to get a second opinion.
          It seems this tiny little miniscule insignificant micro-
          scopic nothing showed up when he did a biopsy.

(SOPHIE opens the envelope and puts a slide under her microscope.)

ED: It's not a great picture of me. *(Pause as SOPHIE looks in her microscope)* My cells aren't my best feature. *(His concern shows)* Sophie, talk.

SOPHIE: *(She is thrown—doesn't know how to talk to him)* It's hard to explain in lay terms.

ED: Hum a few bars and I'll play it.

SOPHIE: *(Playing for time before she says anything to him)* Eddie—

ED: Level with me, Sophie.

SOPHIE: *(Very professional; hiding her feelings)* It's a form of Leukoplakia that's developed into a cigarette-related...

ED: Cancer.

(LUCY enters in LIMBO. SOPHIE and ED continue their conversation in SOPHIE'S lab as LUCY reacts to the news as though hearing it for the first time)

LUCY (IN LIMBO):
SAY SOMETHING FUNNY...

SOPHIE: *(To ED, in the lab)* I've been doing this a long time...

LUCY (IN LIMBO):
GOOD FOR A LAUGH...

SOPHIE (IN HER LAB):
...and I'm afraid it's not an easy one, Ed.

LUCY (IN LIMBO):

          FIRE AT WILL
          DON'T STOP UNTIL
          I'M DOUBLED IN HALF ...

ED: I quit right after *A Chorus Line* opened.

SOPHIE: You smoked for over twenty years. But there's a lot
          that can be done.

  (LEHMAN enters in a separate LIMBO from LUCY)

LEHMAN (IN LIMBO):
          GO FOR THE BIG ONE
          SHOOT ME THE WHOLE BOUQUET ...

ED: Like when you're working on a show, Soph, you can
          always fix the second act.

SOPHIE: The second act's trouble, Ed ...

LUCY (IN LIMBO):
          GET UP AND GIT ME

LEHMAN (IN LIMBO):
          SET UP AND HIT ME

LEHMAN AND LUCY (IN SEPARATE LIMBOS):
          GOING AWAY ...

SOPHIE: But there are new treatments coming out every day.

ED: Ya know, all of a sudden, elevators seem like a cinch.

SOPHIE: (Reaching out to him affectionately.) Eddie—

ED: *(Pulling away)* Nothing's changed. I'm not talking to
          you.

(ED exits. SOPHIE sings to LEHMAN and LUCY.)

SOPHIE: *(A prayer)*
            MAKE IT A WITTY
            MAKE IT A WISE
            LET'S HAVE A JOKE
            I'M GOING BROKE
            FROM WATCHING YOUR EYES

(FELICIA enters)

FELICIA: MAKE MINE THE DOUBLE SPECIAL,
            PLEASE, ON RYE
            SAY SOMETHING FUNNY
            RIGHT ON THE MONEY
            SAY SOMETHING FUNNY
            TRY

(BOBBY enters)

BOBBY: He's faking, right? It's a joke, right?
            HA-HA-HA-HA-HA
            HA-HA-HA-HA-HA

(MONA and CHARLEY enter)

ALL: GOING AND GOING AND GOING AND GOING
            AND *(Angry)* GOD, WHAT A LAUGH!
            OH, COULDN'T YOU JUST DIE?

SOPHIE, LUCY, FELICIA, MONA:
            SAY SOMETHING FUNNY ...

BOBBY, LEHMAN, CHARLEY:
            SAY SOMETHING FUNNY ...

ALL: 'TIL ... I ... CRY

(ED appears in LIMBO.*)*

ED: WHEN THE DAWN BREAKS IN 2001,
           I WON'T BE HERE—

(LIGHTS CHANGE and take us to)

SCENE 8

THE BMI WORKSHOP, 1986

(Alone onstage, ED *uses the audience as his classroom)*

ED: Lehman's in London, so he asked me to take over
           today's class. So I thought this might be a good
           opportunity to go over some of Lehman's "rules," that
           we're never supposed to forget but somehow are the
           first to go. Oh, yeah—I threw in one of my own as
           well.

           Rule Number 1: Be interesting. If you're working on
           a song and it somehow sounds stangely familiar, it's
           probably been written before. Drop it. Start again.

           Rule Number 2: Be a perfectionist. May I remind you,
           "tame" and "lane" do NOT rhyme. "Rake" and "lakes"
           are NOT perfect rhymes. "Moon" and "June" rhyme,
           but it's a cliché.

           Rule Number 3: Learn from me. Songs you write
           alone. Musicals, you write with people. Learn from
           them.

           Rule Number 4: In songwriting, as in life, the most
           important thing is *(a beat)*—everything.

(MUSIC IN, and the LIGHTS CHANGE to indicate that we are inside ED*'s head now:)*

> WHEN THE DAWN BREAKS IN 2001 I WON'T BE
>   THERE
> WHEN THE DAWN BREAKS IN 2001 I'LL BE
>   GONE
> AND THE DEEDS I'M NOT DOING HAD
>   BETTER BE DONE
> AND THE WARS I AM LOSING HAD BETTER BE
>   WON

(As ED *continues,* LEHMAN *wheels on a hospital bed. The scene changes to A HOSPITAL ROOM)*

> WHEN THE DAWN BREAKS IN 2001,
> I'LL BE FINISHED
> WHEN THE BELL RINGS
> I HAD BETTER HAVE NOTHING TO ADD
> WITH MY HEAD HELD HIGH
> AND A FRIGHTENING GLEAM IN MY EYE
> AND EXPECTED BY NO ONE AT ALL
> I WILL LEAVE THE BALL

SCENE 9

A HOSPITAL ROOM

ST. VINCENT'S HOSPITAL, 1987

(By the end of the song, ED *is in bed writing, listening to a baseball game on the radio.)*

RADIO ANNOUNCER (VO):
> *(Actual baseball game)*... Bottom of the ninth—bases loaded—the Mets have two men out—three-two count on Mookie Wilson. And the pitch—

(Stadium noises and crowd cheers continue under, as LUCY *enters)*

LUCY: Ed?

ED: *(agitated)* Turn off the radio, Lucy. I can't think with that thing on.

LUCY: Ed—it's the ninth inning—

(LUCY turns off the radio.)

ED: Thanks. Did you forget to bring more yellow pads?

LUCY: Of course not.

(She takes a pack of pads out of her bag and puts them on the bed)

ED: *(realizing he's treating her badly)* I should have known. Hey, you know what I hate most?

LUCY: What?

ED: I've come to need you.

LUCY: Don't worry. I won't tell anybody your guilty secret.

ED: I'll deny it anyway.

LUCY: Sophie's outside. She waiting to see you.

ED: Never. She's a traitor. Benedict Arnold.

LUCY: Please—she's been here every day this week.

ED: NO!

LUCY: Your favorite word. She asked me to tell you . . .

ED: No! Please. I'm glad you're here. I want you to hear something—

LUCY: You okay? You look tired.

ED: I had a restless night. Sit by the window.

(LUCY *sits near the window.*)

So I can see you. Hair, Luce.

LUCY: *(Adjusting her hair)* Okay?

ED: Okay. You know how I've been struggling with the end of *Gallery?* Never could figure out what all the songs added up to? Well, in the middle of the night, I think I found something. Anyway, it's closer. So. Harold comes to the last room in the gallery, and it's filled with amazing self-portraits he's never seen before, by artists he's never heard of before. Pietro Frasconati, Louisette Tristan, Herman Cherry. None of them became famous, but Harold realizes that's totally unimportant. The only thing that matters is that they spent day after day painting. It's the doing! That's all there is. Now, Harold, finally unafraid, races home to write what he hopes will be his own self-portrait. He sings it, kinda late in the show as it turns out, to the woman who has put up with him through all his impossible everythings.

I'D LOVE FOR YOU TO KNOW ME WELL
TO SEE ME FALLING INTO PLACE

TO SEE THE FACE BEHIND THE FACE
BEHIND THE FACE

I'D LOVE FOR YOU TO SEE ME CLEAR
WITH ALL MY VIRTUES AND MY LIES
WITH ALL THE PLEASURE AND THE PAIN
AROUND THE EYES

I WANT THE OPPORTUNITY
TO SHOW YOU
THE WHOLE DAMN DISPLAY,
TO OPEN LIKE A FLOWER
AND TO KNOW YOU
WILL STAY

I WISH THAT YOU WOULD TAKE ME HOME
AND TAKE THE TIME TO WORK ME OUT,
TO SAY "YES, THERE HE IS.
YES, THAT'S WHAT HE'S ABOUT!
THE JOY OF HIM . . . THE SILLINESS . . .
THE HELL"
I'D LOVE FOR YOU TO KNOW ME VERY WELL

(LEHMAN *enters and wheels* ED *offstage as the rest of the* COM-
PANY *gathers around* LUCY *for the reading of the Will.*)

SCENE 10

THE MEMORIAL, THE SHUBERT THEATRE, 1988

LUCY: *(Reading the will)* "I direct my friend, Lucy Chap-
             rakowski, to read the following list of bequests . . ."

             "Article 1. Several years ago, I made a promise that I
             wish to fulfill, by using royalties to *A Chorus Line* to

create a foundation, to encourage and benefit young songwriters who aspire to write for the theater—a highly endangered species.

"Article 2. I wrote a bunch of songs that are growing mold in the proverbial trunk near my piano. And it is my wish to leave these songs which I value most, to the people I value most.

(ED *re-enters to listen to the reading*)

"I bequeath to my mentor Lehman Engel, 'Charm Song.' To Charley, who loves the workshop, I leave 'Fridays At Four.' The song 'Mona' I leave to Mona— no explanation needed. To Felicia, musical entrepreneur sine qua non, I leave 'Don't Do It Again.' Go to it. 'One More Beautiful Song' I leave to Bobby, to inspire him to continue improving his music and lyrics."

BOBBY: I can live with that.

LUCY: "To my dear Lucy, who has the great gift of 'connecting,' I leave 'I Choose You.' Article 3 ... "

(LUCY *continues M.O.S, as* SOPHIE *enters quietly, unseen by all but* ED.)

SOPHIE: Hi, Eddie.

ED: I told you not to come.

SOPHIE: And you thought I'd listen?

ED: You're late.

SOPHIE: I've been standing at the back. With the legions of other friends you're not speaking to.

ED: Good place for you.

SOPHIE: Now listen, you misunderstood what I said—

ED: Don't start in—Ya know the expression "rest in peace?"—

SOPHIE: You've got to hear me. It's like baseball. You were sitting on the bench too long. I just wanted you to get up to bat. And what I said ... Oh, Eddie. I've loved the sound of your music ever since I was a kid and I am not about to change my mind now. You are a wonderful songwriter.

ED: Was.

SOPHIE: You are. You always will be.

ED: Truth?

SOPHIE: Truth.

ED: Well, I never would have been if it weren't for you. And that's the truth.

    (LUCY's LIGHT BRIGHTENS.)

LUCY: "Article 4. It is my wish, that if I survive until Valentine's Day—my favorite holiday—that Dr. Sophie Callan will be forgiven, and reinstated in my will."

SOPHIE: Ed, that's tomorrow.

ED: Timing was never my strong suit.

LUCY: "But if I go weeks or days or hours earlier, that'd be okay too. Sophie never stopped telling me the truth.

You could hate somebody for that."

(SOPHIE *laughs lightly and* LUCY *notices her.*)

Sophie! I'm so glad you're—Come here . . .

(SOPHIE *joins* LUCY.)

"So, to Sophie, a better friend than I ever deserved, my song 'The Next Best Thing To Love,' as she was and always will be its inspiration."

(*To* SOPHIE) Sophie, read the rest. Please.

SOPHIE: "And to all of my friends, I leave the song 'Self-Portrait.' It is my wish that my friends will arrange for the songs to be performed, preferably in a large building, in a central part of town, in a dark room, as part of a play, with a lot of people listening—"

ALL: —who have all paid a great deal to get in.

SOPHIE: "But if the songs are sung for the love of them, I will probably be content."

SOPHIE, LUCY & ED:
              Probably.

SOPHIE: I'D LOVE FOR YOU TO KNOW ME WELL
              TO SEE ME FALLING INTO PLACE
              TO SEE THE FACE BEHIND THE FACE
              BEHIND THE FACE . . .

BOBBY: It wasn't the money.

CHARLEY: He never even understood money.

(THE COMPANY *all sing to each other, forming a new family without* ED.*)*

SOPHIE & BOBBY:
> I'D LOVE FOR YOU TO SEE ME CLEAR
> WITH ALL MY VIRTUES AND MY LIES
> WITH ALL THE PLEASURE AND THE PAIN
> AROUND THE EYES . . .

FELICIA: Who can say whose life is successful? Don't look at me.

SOPHIE, BOBBY, FELICIA:
> I WANT THE OPPORTUNITY TO SHOW YOU
> THE WHOLE DAMN DISPLAY!

SOPHIE, BOBBY, FELICIA, LEHMAN:
> TO OPEN LIKE A FLOWER AND TO KNOW YOU
> WILL STAY.

LUCY: You know, in a funny way, he got what he wanted.
> I WISH THAT YOU WOULD TAKE ME HOME
> AND TAKE THE TIME TO WORK ME OUT

MONA: TO SAY "YES, THERE HE IS."

CHARLEY, BOBBY, LUCY, MONA:
> "YES, THAT'S WHAT HE'S ABOUT!"

SOPHIE: THE JOY OF HIM . . .
LEHMAN: THE SILLINESS . . .

FELICIA: THE HELL

ALL (INCLUDING ED):
> I'D LOVE FOR YOU TO KNOW ME VERY WELL . . .

(BOBBY holds up the baseball that won the '69 World Series for the Mets and he throws it to ED . . .)

BOBBY: Hey, Buddy—Catch!

(A spot on ED as he reaches up and catches the ball—and beams.)

THE CURTAIN DESCENDS

END

ABOUT THE AUTHORS

EDWARD KLEBAN (Music, Lyrics) was the lyricist of *A Chorus Line*, for which he won the 1975 Tony, The Pulitzer Prize, and The Drama Desk and Olivier Awards. Mr. Kleban's score for *A Class Act* was nominated for the 2001 Tony and Drama Desk Awards, and also received an Obie Award. Mr. Kleban was a graduate of the High School of Music and Art, and of Columbia College, where he wrote the music for the Varsity Show of 1960, with a book by Terrence McNally. In the 1960s, he was a record producer in the heyday of Columbia Records. His musical, *Gallery*, for which he wrote both music and lyrics, was given a workshop at The Public Theater in 1980. The score of *A Class Act* is comprised of songs from *Gallery*, as well as songs from several unfinished Kleban musicals, including *Scandal*, the last Michael Bennett show. Mr. Kleban was a longtime member of Lehman Engel's BMI Musical Theatre Workshop. During the 1980's, he carried on Mr. Engel's tradition and taught songwriting in the workshop. He died in 1987, at the age of 48. The Kleban Foundation, created according to his will, awards grants totaling up to $200,000 a year to aspiring theater lyricists and librettists.

LINDA KLINE (Book) received a 2001 Tony nomination for Best Book for a Musical for *A Class Act*. Ms. Kline wrote the book for *My Heart Is in the East*, produced by The Jewish Repertory Theatre, and for *Cut the Ribbons*, produced at Eighty Eight's (1992 MAC nomination). She co-wrote the book for Theatreworks, U.S.A.'s musical, *The Secret Garden*. Her play, *The Laundry Workers Present Hatpin Bessie*, was produced by the Westbeth Playwrights Feminist Collective. She was head writer of ABC-TV's *FYI* starring Hal Linden (Emmy nomination), and she was a staff writer for *Captain Kangaroo*. She was a member of Lehman Engel's libretto class at The BMI Musical Theatre Workshop.

LONNY PRICE (Book) Lonny Price directed, co-authored and starred in *A Class Act*, first at Manhattan Theatre Club and then on Broadway, where it was nominated for five Tony Awards, including Best Musical and Best Book. After staging a new, pre-Broadway production of *Finian's Rainbow* this past season, Mr. Price directed the New York Philharmonic's *Sweeney Todd*, starring Patti LuPone and George Hearn at Avery Fisher Hall, which he re-staged in San Francisco and Chicago and filmed for a special Halloween broadcast on PBS. He recently directed Eli Wallach in Jeff Baron's *Visiting Mr. Green* and staged the Lincoln Center Theatre concert version of *Annie Get Your Gun* starring Patti LuPone and Peter Gallagher. He also directed Ms. LuPone and Mr.

Gallagher in *Pal Joey* for Encores! He supervised the remounting of Athol Fugard's *Valley Song* for the Manhattan Theatre Club, directed the off-Broadway revivals of the Bock/Harnick/Yellen *The Rothschilds* and the Marc Blitzstein/Joe Stein collaboration *Juno* for the Vineyard Theatre (both nominated for Outer Critics' Circle Awards), as well as Jules Feiffer's *Grown Ups*. On Broadway, he directed Joan Rivers in *Sally Marr . . . and Her Escorts*, which he co-authored with Ms. Rivers and Erin Sanders.

Mr. Price has appeared on and off-Broadway in a variety of plays and musicals, including *A Class Act*, '*Master Harold' . . . and the boys, Merrily We Roll Along, Burn This, Rags, The Immigrant*, and *Falsettoland*, receiving Obie, Theatre World, and Dramalogue awards. He toured the United States and Canada playing Jimmy Durante in the musical *Durante* and also played the title role in two different musical adaptations of *The Apprenticeship of Duddy Kravitz*, the first with a score by Jerry Leiber and Mike Stoller and the second by Alan Menken.

His most prominent film role was as the slimy Neil in *Dirty Dancing*; on TV, he has guested on *The Golden Girls, Dear John* (as Judd Hirsch's son) and several episodes of *Law and Order*. Mr. Price received an Emmy nomination for his work on ABC's *One Life to Live*, where he was a director for four seasons.

He is the Artistic Director of Musical Theatre Works, a not-for-profit theater dedicated to the development of new musicals for the stage.